BIBLE ENCYCLOPEDIA FOR CHILDREN

BIBLE ENCYCLOPEDIA
FOR CHILDREN

by **CECIL NORTHCOTT**
designed and illustrated by **DENIS WRIGLEY**

THE WESTMINSTER PRESS · PHILADELPHIA

INTRODUCTION

This "Bible Encyclopedia for Children" deals with the chief people, the main events, and the leading ideas of the Bible.

In writing the text the aim has been to provide the basic information about the Bible, and to guide children towards finding out more through reading the Bible themselves.

The entries in the "Encyclopedia" are accompanied by Bible references and the illustrations have been so chosen and displayed that the "Encyclopedia" becomes a readable book in itself as well as a source of information.

The facts in the "Encyclopedia" are the ones which are central to the Bible story and help to build up for children a view of the Bible as the Word of God.

In the main, the Bible references in the "Encyclopedia" are to the King James, or Authorized Version of the Bible, but when this is varied the reference is to the Revised Standard Version.

The editor and publishers are grateful to the many co-operators in this enterprise, who have advised on the general plan and have read the entries.

In particular they wish to thank Mr. G. H. Lankester Harding, C.B.E., F.S.A., Fellow of University College, London, and for twenty years Director of the Department of Antiquities in Jordan, for his skilled advice in connection with the illustrations.

Printed in Great Britain

Published in the U.S.A. by The Westminster Press, ®, Philadelphia 7, Pennsylvania

AARON. We first meet Aaron in the Bible when God commands him to be chief speaker, on behalf of his brother Moses, to the people of Israel. It was this gift of speech which led to Aaron's appointment as Israel's priest. Moses presented him with beautiful and richly decorated priest's garments in gold, blue, purple and scarlet. The two brothers worked closely together for the benefit of the people. *Exodus 4. 10ff; 28; 30.*

ABBA. A word of the Aramaic language spoken in the time of Christ meaning 'father'. Jesus used it when speaking of God as his Father. *Mark 14. 36.*

ABEDNEGO. During the captivity of the Jews in Babylon three young Jews—Shadrach, Meshach and Abednego—worked in the household of King Nebuchadnezzar. The king ordered them to worship his gods but they refused to deny the one true God. In his anger the king had them thrown into a blazing furnace to be burnt to death. God was with them in the furnace, and to the king's great surprise they came out unharmed. *Daniel 3. 19–30.*

ABEL. Second son of Adam and Eve, a shepherd who was killed by his elder brother Cain. *Genesis 4. 1–8.*

ABIGAIL. It was the time of the shearing of the sheep in the Carmel area of Palestine and Nabal, Abigail's husband, had three thousand sheep and a thousand goats: the news of the great shearing spread to the camp of David who sent a group of his young men with his greetings to Nabal. Nabal rudely turned them away and refused to give them food. But his wife Abigail—not only beautiful but hospitable—packed them up a huge supply of food and rode over the hills herself to David's camp to apologize for her husband's rudeness. When she got home she found her husband drunk and he died soon afterwards in a fit. David, charmed by her looks and her conduct, married her. *1 Samuel 25.*

ABISHAI. Amongst the brave and devoted men who served David, none was braver than his nephew Abishai. One night, he and David crept into King Saul's camp. Saul was fast asleep. He was at their mercy. 'Let me spear him to death,' whispered Abishai. 'No,' said David, 'we must not kill the Lord's anointed!' David contented himself with taking Saul's spear and cruse of water. Abishai was surprised at his uncle's merciful act. He and all David's men never forgot it, and neither did King Saul. *1 Samuel 26.*

ABNER. 'Why should we go on fighting like this?' cried Abner, the commander of Saul's army to Joab, David's captain. 'It always brings bitterness in the end' he said. So Joab blew the trumpet of peace and Abner and his men were allowed to pass safely over the River Jordan. A stern fighter himself Abner had a generous heart. He offered to help win all Israel to the side of David, but was killed himself before he could put the plan into action. *2 Samuel 2 and 3.*

ABRAHAM. Abraham was an old man when he came wandering across the desert lands of Mesopotamia with his flocks and herds seeking good pasture in the land of Canaan. Beneath the wide skies and stars he marched and camped under the guidance of God. He was rich in cattle and servants and generous and kind to his friends. God made three promises to him: that he would be the father of a great nation, that this nation would be God's special people, and that a son, Isaac, would be born to Sarah his wife in her old age. Abraham's faith was severely tested when God asked him to kill Isaac as a sacrifice. God saved Isaac but Abraham's readiness to obey marked him out as a man obedient to God. Abraham's faithfulness in following God makes Paul in his letter to the Romans (4. 12) call him 'father of us all'. *Genesis 11–22.*

'Abraham went as the Lord had told him'

ABSALOM. The handsome, third son of King David who led a rebellion against his father. Caught by his hair in the branches of an oak tree—after his defeat in battle—Absalom was killed by David's troops. David had given instructions that Absalom should not be injured and was grief-stricken at the news. *2 Samuel 18. 32–33.*

ACHAN. When the people of Israel invaded the land of Canaan they attacked the strong, rich town of Ai. Every man was warned by the leader Joshua not to steal from the homes of the people as everything belonged to God. But Achan was tempted and secretly hid money and clothing in his tent. He confessed his sin and was led out to a lonely place and stoned to death. *Joshua 7. 19–26.*

ACTS OF THE APOSTLES. The New Testament book which records the activities of the disciples and friends of Jesus. It describes how the Christian church started and grew, and especially relates the exploits of the great apostle Paul. It is the second part of Luke's history of which his Gospel is the first part. *Acts of the Apostles.*

ADAM. When God created human life he made it out of dust of the earth, and called the first man *Adam* which means *ground*. *Genesis 1 and 2.*

ADRIA. As Paul was sailing to Rome his ship was caught in a great storm in the sea of Adria not far from the island of Malta. The huge waves tossed the ship so dangerously that the crew had to throw the cargo overboard, and only Paul's courage saved them from being drowned. Adria is the ancient name for the Adriatic Sea. *Acts 27. 27.*

ADULLAM. In the limestone cliffs of this town David found a secret cave where he and his followers hid from King Saul and there plotted against him. *1 Samuel 22. 1.*

AENEAS. For eight years Aeneas who lived in the town of Lydda had been ill. He was so paralysed that he could not move but Peter came to see him and in the name of Jesus gave him power to get up and walk. *Acts 9. 32–34.*

AGRIPPA. Two men faced each other in the court of justice. One was a judge, King Agrippa, a member of the ruling family of Herod, and the other the prisoner—Paul. As the prisoner spoke the judge listened spellbound and felt a strange moving of his own heart. 'You almost persuade me to be a Christian,' he said. 'I would to God you were,' replied Paul. *Acts 26. 1–32.*

AHAB (see also *Elijah*). King of Israel from 869–850 B.C. Ahab was a king who knew the right but failed to do it. Egged on by his wicked wife Jezebel he built temples to false gods until Elijah, the prophet, challenged him to show who was the stronger—Elijah's God or the gods of Ahab. Elijah assembled the people on the top of Mount Carmel, and in a dramatic act they saw the bullock of Elijah's sacrifice burnt up in a great flame of fire while the bullocks of Ahab's priests remained unconsumed. At the end of his reign Ahab repented of his misdeeds and as the Bible says, 'He went softly' always in fear of the prophet Elijah's anger. *1 Kings 18.*

ALABASTER (see also *Anointing*). As Iesus sat in the house of his friends in Bethany a woman came with a flask, made of the precious alabaster stone, filled with perfume. She broke the neck of the flask and to everyone's surprise poured the perfume on his head as a sign of her love for him. *Mark 14. 3.*

ALEXANDRIA. A great sea-port in Egypt and the home port of the big ships which carried grain to Rome. *Acts 27. 6.*

ALPHA AND OMEGA. When the New Testament writers wished to talk of the things which were 'first and last' or the 'beginning and the end' they often used these first and last letters of the Greek alphabet. *Revelation 1. 8–11.*

ALTAR. Noah, Abraham, Isaac, Jacob, Moses, Joshua and Elijah all built altars in the places where God had spoken to them. These altars of sacrifice were probably short stone pillars, but later in Solomon's day the altar was built more elaborately at the Temple. *Genesis 8. 20; 12. 7; 35. 1.*

AMALEKITES. On the top of a hill in the Desert of Sinai Moses stood with his arms raised praying for the people of Israel in their fight with the fierce warrior people the Amalekites. But he was old and soon grew tired. His arms fell by his side and then the Israelite fighters weakened. So a seat was made for him on the hill and Aaron and Hur stood by Moses' side holding up the old man's arms until the sunset and the battle against the Amalekites was won. In thanksgiving for the victory Moses built an altar on the spot. *Exodus 17. 8–16.*

AMEN. This is a Hebrew word meaning 'surely'. Jesus used it, when he said 'Verily, verily, I say unto you'. In the Book of Revelation Jesus himself is referred to as 'The Amen', an expressive way of saying that Jesus Christ is the sure and final truth. *Revelation 3. 14.*

AMMONITES. Descendants of Lot's younger son, the Ammonites were regarded as relatives of the Israelites, but they were often enemies. When the walls of Jerusalem were re-built in the 5th century B.C. Nehemiah the prophet, who led the great enterprise, was jeered at by the Ammonites. They mocked him. 'Even a fox running over the stones will knock them down' they shouted. 'You can't build the walls again.' But Nehemiah went on with the job in spite of the Ammonites' opposition and built the city walls to the glory of God. *Nehemiah 2 and 4.*

Sometimes a simple stone—the altar was for sacrifice and incense burning

AMOS. Nearly eight hundred years before Jesus Amos went out into the countryside near Jerusalem to call the people to obey God. He was a 'prophet' and called on the people to practise their faith in their daily lives. He preached truth, honesty, and righteousness. He said that God wished to see these virtues in men's actions. No amount of outward religious ceremonial was a substitute for them. To Amos God was a Holy God and required his worshippers to be holy too in the way they lived. *Book of Amos.*

7

**Anchors up at Alexandria—
and over the sea to Rome**

A winged and kingly figure of the Babylonian period

ANANIAS. With Sapphira, his wife, Ananias, who was an active member of the church, sold land and told the apostle Peter that he had given *all* the money to the church. Peter knew that Ananias had kept back some of the money for himself. Peter said, 'You have lied to God', and Ananias fell down dead. *Acts 5. 1–6.*

ANDREW. As Jesus was walking by the Sea of Galilee he saw two fishermen brothers, Peter and Andrew, mending their fishing nets. He called them to follow him, which they did at once for Andrew had heard of Jesus and had told Peter about him. He was sure that here was the man they were all looking for, and ever after Andrew was always eager to bring his friends to Jesus. *Matthew 4. 18; John 1. 40.*

ANGELS. The Bible speaks in many places of angels as messengers of God, 'spirits' that go on God's errands between heaven and earth. They are thought of as swift and beautiful, and help to show the loveliness of God himself. *Acts 6. 15.*

ANOINTING (see also *Alabaster*). As an outward sign of holiness and purity people in the Bible were often 'anointed' on the head, or breast, with oil or perfume. Places and utensils were treated in the same way. They became God's people and God's places. The anointing was taken to mean that God favoured them and wished to use them in his service. When Samuel chose David to be the future leader of God's people he went down to the farm of Jesse —David's father—and there with all the family round him he 'anointed' David with the 'horn of oil'. From that day onwards David was known as the one who had the mark of God on him. *1 Samuel 16.*

ANTIOCH. Near the sea coast three hundred miles north of Israel Antioch was the city where the followers of Jesus were first called 'Christians'. From there Paul set out on his missionary journeys. The site of another ancient Antioch is now in Turkey. *Acts 11. 19.*

APOLLOS. 'Who then do you really belong to?' asked Paul of the Christians in the city of Corinth. 'Some of you say you are for Paul and some for Apollos. But we are both ministers of Christ. We work together for Christ.' Apollos, like Paul, was a Jew and an eloquent preacher for Christ and it may be that some liked him in preference to Paul. Some scholars think he wrote one of the most wonderful books in the Bible—the Epistle to the Hebrews. *1 Corinthians 3. 4–11.*

APOSTLE. Jesus himself is called 'the Apostle', the one who is 'sent' from God. Those who are 'sent' to preach and teach are called 'apostles' and the twelve men who were the leaders of the church are called 'the apostles'. *Luke 6. 13; 1 Corinthians 4. 9; Hebrews 3. 1.*

AQUILA. When Paul came to Corinth he stayed in the home of Aquila and Priscilla, his wife, both faithful Christians. Like them Paul was a tent-maker skilled in the use of needle and thread. But Aquila also shared Paul's love of travel and wherever he went he was hospitable, generous and kind to members of the churches. Paul gave his friends a lovely name, 'My helpers in Christ Jesus'. *Acts 18. 1–3; Romans 16. 3.*

ARK, NOAH'S. When the great flood came upon the earth Noah, according to the Bible story, was told by God to make an ark to float on the waters. He was instructed how to design its rooms and how to keep the ark dry during the flood which lasted one hundred and fifty days. There was space for Noah and his family and two of every sort of living creature. The ark floated dry and warm and from its window Noah looked out every day to see the waters fall away. When a little dove returned with an olive leaf in its beak Noah knew that the waters were subsiding. God's promise to save him was fulfilled. *Genesis 6–9.*

ARK, OF THE COVENANT. In the long journey of the people of Israel across the desert into the land of Canaan they carried a sacred ark. It was a beautifully made box of acacia wood covered in gold and carried on golden poles. In it was a copy of the Ten Commandments. The ark was always a sign of God's presence, and the symbol of divine guidance. *Exodus 25. 10.*

Babylon, famed for its massive and decorated city gates (p. 10)

ASCENSION, THE. After Jesus had risen from the dead he came again to see his disciples before he returned to His Father's presence. He then called his disciples together and gave them his commands to preach the good news about himself in every part of the world. While he was speaking a cloud covered him and Jesus 'ascended into heaven'. They all gazed in wonder and knew that God's power had worked a miracle. *Acts 1. 9.*

ASSYRIA. To the north-east of Palestine lay the land of Assyria, a mighty empire centred round the great rivers Euphrates and Tigris. Its power lasted from 1000–

Most precious, carefully guarded, and carried wherever the people went—the Israelite Ark of the Covenant

612 B.C. in the area now called Mesopotamia. Nineveh was the chief city of Assyria. Confined to their little land so close to the sea on one side and the desert on the other the Israelites were often afraid of attack by the Assyrians. On a number of occasions Israelites were carried off in captivity to Assyria and their kings had to pay tribute. *2 Kings 18.*

ATHENS. 'Ye men of Athens,' said Paul, 'you are very superstitious. It is God who gives life to all things, and not the gods you worship.' That bold speech was made in A.D. 50 in the heart of the capital of Greece, a world centre of philosophical learning. *Acts 17. 22.*

ATONEMENT. To Christians 'atonement' means 'making at one' with God. Jesus made that clear for all men in his own life and death. He showed men that the heart of God is love. By his sacrifice for us our sins are forgiven. In the Old Testament

9

the high priest made the 'sacrifice' for the people's sins in the 'holy of holies'. In the New Testament Jesus himself makes the 'atonement' as both high priest and 'sacrifice'. *John 3. 16; Romans 5. 11.*

ATONEMENT, DAY OF. To the Jewish people the Day of Atonement is the most sacred day of their year. By prayer in the Temple and fasting they remember God's goodness to them and ask for his forgiveness of their sins. In the 'holy of holies' the high priest offers a blood sacrifice as an 'atonement' for the people's sins. This ritual is linked to the 'atonement' of Christ in the Epistle to the Hebrews.
Leviticus 23. 27; Hebrews 9.

B **BAAL** (see also *Ahab*). When the Israelites came into Canaan they found many local

'Barbarians' on Malta! They rushed to help the shipwrecked crew including Paul

gods, or *baals*. Every piece of land had its *baal*, meaning master, or owner. Against the worship of these *baals* they set the worship of the one true God.
1 Kings 18. 18.

BABEL, TOWER OF. In the days of ancient Babylon the people were great builders and prided themselves on what they could do with bricks and mortar. 'Let us build a tower,' they said, 'tall enough to reach right up to heaven, and then our names will be famous throughout the world.' But God saw beyond the great tower to the pride of the people, and scattered them into many places so that they began to speak in different languages. The

exact place of the great tower at Babylon is not known, but the name *Babel* has come to mean confusion in speaking, a *babel* of languages. *Genesis 11. 1–9.*

BABYLON. One of the wonder cities of the ancient world, about fifty miles south of modern Baghdad in Iraq. Babylon had huge walls, massive gates and a great temple. Its famous king, Nebuchadnezzar, often boasted of his wonderful city, and to it the Jews were carried in captivity. But the great prophets of the Old Testament, Isaiah and Jeremiah, prophesied that even Babylon would be captured and destroyed, and so it was by the Persians (five hundred years before Christ), and only its ruins remain today. *Daniel 4.*

BALAAM. In the days when the people of Israel were moving into the Promised Land, a 'prophet' Balaam rode off one day on his donkey to negotiate with their enemies the people of Moab. As he rode along the donkey suddenly stopped and swerved off the road. Baalam beat the donkey to keep her on the road, but the donkey swerved again and at last lay down, and in spite of Balaam's beatings refused to get up. The donkey had seen the vision of an angel, a warning to Balaam that his journey was not pleasing to God. Balaam realized that his donkey was wiser than he was and turned to go back. 'No,' said the angel, 'go on but watch how you go and be careful what you say to these men of Moab.' *Numbers 22.*

BALM (see also *Gilead*). A sweet smelling spice which came from Gilead, the hilly, wooded land across the River Jordan to the north of the Dead Sea. It was used for healing purposes, and today Arabs use a similar spice for flavouring their coffee, sweets and chewing gum.
Jeremiah 8. 22; 46. 11.

BAPTISM. Baptism is one of the great acts linking men with God. It points to

what God has done for us and forward to a life of faith in him. Water is used as a sign in this baptism. Jesus was baptized in the River Jordan. Through Jesus comes the 'baptism of the Holy Spirit'. Christian baptism is by water and the spirit. It is a sign of life in Christ and membership in his Church.
Matthew 3. 13; John 3. 5; Acts 2. 38.

BARABBAS. 'Whom will you have?'cried Pilate, 'Jesus or Barabbas?' Stirred up by the chief priests, the crowd shouted 'Barabbas! Let Jesus be crucified.' As Jesus stood before Pontius Pilate, the Roman governor, the crowd surged round the judgment hall during the Feast of the Passover. It was the custom for the governor to release a prisoner on such a festive occasion to please the crowd. The bandit Barabbas was therefore released in preference to Jesus.
Matthew 27. 15–26.

BARBARIANS. As the ship carrying Paul to Italy ran aground on the island of Malta, everybody on board jumped into the sea and struggled to the shore. They wondered how the people on the land would treat them. Paul called the islanders *barbarians* which means *foreigners* or *natives*. They rushed to help the half-drowned men, lighting a fire, cooking food and treating them with much kindness. They were at first frightened to see a snake out of a wood pile fastening on Paul's arm. They were astonished to see him throw it off into the fire with no harm to himself. These barbarians were so impressed that they said Paul was a god. *Acts 28. 1–6.*

'Then Noah sent forth the dove; and she did not return to him any more' (p. 9)

BARNABAS. After his conversion on the road to Damascus, Paul came to Jerusalem to meet the other disciples of Christ. But they were afraid of him—this man who had been a persecutor of Christians. Could he now be their friend? Who would tell of his new character? Barnabas spoke for him, and from then on stood by Paul in his ventures for Christ among the Gentiles. His name means 'son of comfort or consolation' and Luke says he was 'a good man full of the Holy Spirit and faith'.
Acts 9. 27; 11. 22–26.

BARTHOLOMEW. One of the twelve disciples whose name appears in the lists given in the Gospels, but about whom very little is known. Some think he is Nathanael mentioned in John's Gospel (1. 45).
Matthew 10.3.

Belshazzar sees the shadow and the writing on the wall as he feasts in his palace

BARTIMAEUS. 'Thou Son of David have mercy on me.' The cry echoed down the road as Jesus left Jericho and so touched Jesus' heart that he asked for blind Bartimaeus to be brought to him. He jumped up in his excitement, threw off his cloak and

Beds—it might be just a mat on the floor—or an elegant couch

ran to Jesus. 'Lord,' he said, 'give me my sight,' and so powerful was his faith that his eyes were opened and he followed Jesus down the road.   *Mark 10. 46–52.*

BATHSHEBA. The mother of Solomon, who became king of Israel after his father David. Before becoming the wife of David Bathsheba was married to Uriah, a soldier in the army of Israel. David saw Bathsheba and fell in love with her. Bathsheba's husband, Uriah, was killed when David ordered him to the front of the battle.
2 Samuel 12.

BEANS. It might mean peanuts. Sometimes a substitute for grain in time of famine.   *2 Samuel 17. 28; Ezekiel 4. 9.*

BEATITUDES.—see *Sermon on the Mount*.

BED. The bed of a poor man was usually a simple reed mat. In rich homes people had couches to sleep on with warm clothes for the cold nights. *Mark 2. 4.*

BEELZEBUB (or *Baalzebub*). One of the 'local gods' of the Old Testament. Sometimes called 'lord of the high place'. In the New Testament, Jesus is accused by the Pharisees of using the power of this god, whom they identified as Satan, to cast out evil spirits. *Matthew 12. 24–28.*

BEERSHEBA. In Old Testament times Beersheba was an important place on the route midway between the Mediterranean and the southern part of the Dead Sea. Traders going into Egypt stopped at Beersheba and the herdsmen with their cattle liked the deep cool water of its wells. Abraham lived for a time at Beersheba and from there set off on the fateful journey to sacrifice Isaac. The people often described the northern and southern limits of their country with the phrase 'From Dan to Beersheba'. *Judges 20. 1.*

BELIAL. The Bible speaks of a 'son of' Belial to describe a very wicked person. The origin of the word is obscure, but it was the worst that could be said about anyone. It may have been another name for 'Satan' or even 'hell'. *2 Corinthians 6. 15.*

BELLS. Little bells of gold were stitched to the hem of the high priest's dress so that the people could hear him going into the sanctuary. Bells adorned the necks of animals, and were sometimes tied round the necks of children just to let people know where they were. *Exodus 28. 33, 34.*

BELSHAZZAR. In the great palace of King Belshazzar in Babylon in 539 B.C. a feast was laid for a thousand people, and all the king's magnificent gold and silver vessels were displayed. But as they feasted and drank a man's hand appeared like a vast shadow on the wall facing the king's seat and wrote a message on it. The king trembled and grew frightened as the hand wrote out its words. What did they mean? None of the king's wise men could interpret them. Then they remembered Daniel, one of the young captured Israelites. Daniel came and read the writing. 'O Belshazzar,' he said, 'thou art weighed in the balances, and art found wanting. Thy kingdom is finished.' That night Belshazzar was killed and Babylon was captured by the Persians. *Daniel 5.*

BETHANY. The home Jesus loved to go to was in the small village of Bethany—about two miles outside Jerusalem on the Jericho road. There his friends Mary, Martha and their brother, Lazarus, lived.

Bells! bells! To show where everybody was

'Her firstborn son, wrapped in swaddling clothes, laid in a manger' (p. 14)

Their home gave Jesus rest and quiet. It was in the Bethany home that the woman poured out perfume to anoint him; and there Mary sat at his feet listening while Martha was so busy in the house. There Jesus raised Lazarus from the dead, and from Bethany he set out on his triumphal ride into Jerusalem.
Luke 10. 38–42; John 11. 1–44.

BETHEL (see also *Altar*). At Bethel, in the hilly open land twelve miles north of Jerusalem, Abraham, in his wanderings, pitched his tent and built an altar to God. Jacob too began to know God at Bethel. Bethel continued to be respected as a holy place, and today Christians often speak of the 'God of Bethel'. It means 'House of God'. *Genesis 12. 1–9; 35. 1–4.*

BETHESDA, POOL OF. For years the sick man had gone regularly to the Pool of Bethesda in Jerusalem hoping to dip himself into the healing waters of the Pool. But at the moment when the waters were 'troubled' there was no one to help him into the water. He missed his chance as other people got in front of him. But Jesus said to him 'Rise, take up thy bed and walk', and the man immediately felt his legs become strong enough for him to walk easily. *John 5. 1–9.*

BETHLEHEM. The birthplace of Jesus Christ. There in a stable his mother, Mary, was compelled to lie because there was no room in the inn, and the first bed for Jesus was a manger lined with hay. On the Bethlehem hills the shepherds hailed the good news that Christ was born and the Wise Men from the East came to worship him. The name may mean 'house of bread'. It was the old home of Jesus' ancestors—the family of David. *Luke 2. 1–22.*

BETHPHAGE. As Jesus and his disciples walked towards Jerusalem, at the turning point in the road, on the Mount of Olives, Jesus spoke to his disciples. 'Over there,' he said, 'in the village opposite, you will find a colt tied which has never been ridden on. Bring it here.' And so from Bethphage Jesus rode onward to Jerusalem while the people threw their cloaks in front of him and shouted, 'Blessed is he who cometh in the name of the Lord. Hosanna in the highest.' *Matthew 21. 1–11; Luke 19. 28–38.*

BETHSAIDA. After the feeding of the five thousand, Jesus told his disciples to row across the lake to Bethsaida while he dismissed the crowd and went into the hills to pray. Looking out across the lake he saw them rowing hard against the wind and the choppy sea. Then in the hour before the dawn, Jesus came to them walking on the sea. Tired and frightened they thought it was a ghost until Jesus spoke. He got into the boat, the wind ceased and they landed safely at Bethsaida—a town on the north shore of Galilee meaning 'house of fishing'. *Mark 6. 45–52.*

BIBLE (see also *Old* and *New Testaments*). This Greek word meaning 'the books' is used by Christians to describe the sacred writings in which God reveals himself. The Bible is the word of God to men. Its central message is the story of God's love and salvation which progresses through its two sections—the Old and New Testaments—to its climax in the life, death, and resurrection of God's son, Jesus Christ. Although the Bible has many books, it has one message. It is the message to men of God's salvation. That is why the Bible is the book of final authority for all believing Christians. *The Bible.*

BIRTHRIGHT (see also *Esau*). To be the first born son in a Jewish home was to be an important person, and next in authority to the father. The first born always inherited twice as much of his father's property as any other son and he usually succeeded to his father's position. This was considered to be his 'birthright'—that which properly was his by reason of his birth. *Genesis 25. 31; Luke 2. 7.*

BISHOP. In the New Testament a 'bishop is a man who 'oversees' or looks after the people in the churches. He is required to be an honourable man, hospitable, patient, kindly and understanding, a good teacher who knows the meaning of the Christian faith. *1 Timothy 3. 1–7.*

BLASPHEMY. To insult God by word or deed is 'blasphemy'. It is the worst thing men can do. In the Old Testament people who did so were stoned to death. *Leviticus 24. 10–23.*

BLESSING. In the Old Testament this generally means the coming of something 'good' in money, land, or family happiness. But in the New Testament the word is

A boy was always welcome in a Jewish home; the first boy had the 'birthright'

wider in its meaning and includes the good news of the Gospel.
Proverbs 10. 22; Romans 15. 29.

BOANERGES. When Jesus called his first disciples he gave some of them new names such as Simon whom he re-named Peter. Two others, James and John, he called *Boanerges* meaning 'Sons of Thunder'. No reason is given for this but it may have been because Jesus knew their fierce and fiery tempers. Only Mark records the name and he probably well remembered how hot-blooded the two men were, for he

Boaz for his kindness to a foreigner. From their marriage came a son who was grandfather of King David. *Book of Ruth.*

BOOKS. Books such as we know them were not in existence in Bible times. The usual form of 'a book' was a roll, or scroll of papyrus, or of leather or parchment. Such rolls were often written on both sides. *2 Kings 22. 8; 23. 3.*

BOTTLE. 'No one puts new wine into old wine skins,' said Jesus, 'because they

heard about them from their close friend— Simon Peter. *Mark 3. 17.*

BOAZ (see also *Ruth*). All day long the reapers had been at work in the fields of Farmer Boaz at Bethlehem. After the Israelite custom, Boaz allowed young women gleaners to follow behind the reapers and to pick up the stray ears of barley. One of the young women, Ruth, was a stranger to Bethlehem. She came from the land of Moab but Boaz gave strict orders that everyone was to be kind to the foreigner. At threshing time, he also gave Ruth an extra helping of barley. Eventually, he married Ruth. All Bethlehem admired

are certain to burst. You must use new skins.' Biblical bottles were usually made of skins of goats, or sheep, tanned and sewn together, and were hard wearing. Unlike glass bottles, they could crack with age. The warning of Jesus was quickly understood by his listeners. *Matthew 9. 17.*

BREAD. 'Give us this day our daily bread.' When Jesus put the word *bread* into the Lord's Prayer he was using a word that everyone was familiar with. Barley flour, mixed with water and seasoned with salt, was kneaded with fermented dough to make the daily bread. This was baked over the open fire in the shape of round, flat loaves. As the staple food of every home, the word *bread* really meant all kinds of

Boaz said to his young men 'Let her glean among the sheaves. Don't stop her'

15

Biblical books and bottles

food. Jesus himself on the last night of his life took bread and made it the symbol of himself in the Lord's Supper which Christians everywhere observe as he commanded. *Matthew 26. 26–29; John 6. 35–41.*

BRICKS. 'No more straw for the Israelite bricks.' That was the order from Pharaoh in Egypt as the Israelites slaved away under their cruel taskmasters. Every day they had to make so many bricks out of the clay and dry them in the sun. They were given straw to mix with the clay because the straw— as it rotted—helped to bind the brick firmly. Now they had to gather their own straw but still make the same number of bricks. The people rebelled against the order and that rebellion was the first step towards their escape from Egypt. *Exodus 5. 15–19.*

BULRUSH. These tall rushes are found in the rivers and swamps of Bible lands growing as high as twenty feet. From them are made ropes, sandals, baskets; and strips of the rushes — beaten together — make papyrus 'paper'. The baby Moses was found hidden in an ark amongst the bulrushes of the River Nile, and 'adopted' by Pharaoh's daughter. *Exodus 2. 1–10.*

BURIAL. On the evening that Jesus died, Joseph of Arimathea came and asked Pilate for the body to bury in his own new tomb, hewn in the rock. Burial had to be soon after death with the body wrapped in a linen cloth. It was customary for families to have their own burial places, usually outside the town. There were no common burial grounds, or cemeteries, and cremation was never a Jewish practice. *Matthew 27. 57–61.*

BURNING BUSH. 'Moses, Moses, do not come near; put off your shoes from your feet, for this place on which you are standing is holy ground.' It was God's call to the future leader of Israel as he shepherded sheep in the wilderness. The call came from within a burning bush which suddenly burst into flames that did not destroy the bush. Moses heard God speaking to him through the flames, but he hesitated and made excuses for not following the call. But the experience taught him that God was planning to use him as a leader of the Israelites. *Exodus 3. 1–6.*

BURNT OFFERING. Like all ancient peoples the Israelites practised 'sacrifice' or 'burning' as part of their worship. Usually parts of animals were burnt upon the altar as offerings of devotion to God. *1 Kings 3. 4; 2 Chronicles 29. 27.*

C **CAESAR.** Originally associated with a powerful Roman family, the name, Caesar, stood in New Testament times for the imperial authority and power of Rome. As Paul stood before Festus, Caesar's representative in Judaea, he said 'If I have done wrong, if I have done anything for which I deserve to die, then I will be judged by Caesar.' Paul was a Roman citizen and therefore had the right to go to the highest authority in the Empire, the Emperor— Caesar himself in Rome. *Acts 25. 6–12.*

CAESAREA. A city and seaport on the Mediterranean shore about sixty miles from Jerusalem, and the headquarters of the Roman administration of Judaea. *Acts 10. 1.*

CAESAREA-PHILIPPI. 'But who do you say that I am?' That famous question was put to Peter at Caesarea-Philippi, a town

Burning bush— probably of white broom which grew twelve feet high in the wilderness

in the lovely foothills of Mount Hermon across the Jordan from Galilee. Jesus and his disciples were talking together about the various ideas which people had about him. Who was he? Some said he was John the Baptist, others Elijah, or Jeremiah, or one of the prophets. Then Jesus turned and faced the men—especially Peter—and said 'But what about you? Who do you say that I am?' And then came Peter's confident reply, 'You are the Christ, the Son of the Living God.' *Matthew 16. 13–20.*

CAIAPHAS. High Priest of the Jews in the time of Jesus, Caiaphas was the leader of the group which plotted to arrest Jesus, and he was the first judge before whom Jesus came to be tried. It was he who put to Jesus the challenging question, 'Are you the Christ, the Son of God?' to which Jesus answered, 'You have said so', a reply that so infuriated Caiaphas and his council that they cried, 'He deserves death!' *Matthew 26. 57–68.*

CAIN. The elder son of Adam and Eve who became a farmer and murdered his brother Abel. *Genesis 4. 1–10.*

CALVARY. It was on the hill of Calvary that Jesus was crucified, a hill outside Jerusalem. Calvary was probably near a high road, not far from a city gate and near a garden. No one today knows exactly where the spot was. But the name in Latin means 'skull', so the hill Calvary may have been shaped like a skull. *Luke 23. 32–56.*

CANA. A village not far from Nazareth in which Jesus and his mother attended a wedding reception of friends. Cana was famed for its springs of cool water and shady fig-trees. The party was going along very happily when suddenly the bridegroom realized that there was not enough wine in the jars to go round. When Jesus heard about it he told the steward to fill up the jars with water, right to the brim, and when they poured it out—it was wine. The

On Calvary they crucified him— with the criminals

Tools for the carpenter's bench in Nazareth

steward was astonished, and said to the bridegroom 'Usually the good wine comes first at a feast but this is the best of all.' This was the first of the recorded miracles of Jesus. *John 2. 1–11.*

CANAAN. 'Go,' said Moses, 'and see what sort of land it is that God has promised to us.' This was his instruction to the twelve spies representing the twelve tribes of Israel as they started off to spy out the land of Canaan. They went up through the hills from their base at Kadesh-Barnea and into the plain bordering the Mediterranean Sea which is the land of Canaan proper. They found it to be a land of strong cities, prosperous farms with good crops, and they brought back big bunches of grapes. 'It is a land flowing with milk and honey,' they said. Later on Joshua led the people of Israel over the River Jordan into Canaan, which they called the Promised Land. *Numbers 13.*

CANDLE. The candle as we know it was not in use in Bible times. Light came from the 'lamp' which is often referred to as the 'candle'. The lamp was a small flat earthen bowl of oil with a wick floating in it. It gave a very feeble light and needed to be put on a 'stand' to give a good light. 'Don't hide your light,' said Jesus, 'put it on a stand so that all can see.' *Matthew 5. 14–16; Revelation 1. 12–16.*

CAPERNAUM. On the north-west shore of Galilee, Capernaum was a familiar town for Jesus. It was there he called Matthew from sitting at his table in the tax office. Matthew left all and followed him. In Capernaum too lived a Roman Centurion who asked Jesus to heal his servant. 'Just say the word,' he said to Jesus, 'and he will be healed': a faith Jesus marvelled at as he announced the healing. Capernaum was also the home of Peter's wife's mother, and Jesus often came there to talk with the people. *Matthew 8. 8–9.*

18

On guard for Rome!

CAPTIVITY. To take a defeated people into captivity, or exile, was a common custom in Bible times. About six hundred years before Jesus, Nebuchadnezzar, king of Babylon, brought his armies to besiege Jerusalem. For two years the fighting went on until in 587 B.C. the city was captured and its walls destroyed. Hundreds of people were carried off for long years of captivity in Babylon. They were not cruelly treated and some returned to rebuild the Temple and the walls of the city. *2 Kings 25.*

The light, swift chariot for pleasure and for war. Solomon had 1400 of them

CARMEL (see also *Elijah*). As you look down the coast of Palestine on the map you see the hills of the Mount Carmel range jutting out into the sea. The deep wooded hills are a refreshing sight from the hot lands of the plains, and the prophets and preachers of Israel often pointed out to their hearers the beauty of God's creation in Mount Carmel. *Isaiah 35. 1–2.*

CARPENTER. Jesus learned the ancient craft of the carpenter, and became a skilled worker in wood. He was taught his trade by Joseph in the carpenter's shop at Nazareth where he used the saw, the chisel, the drill and the hammer to make chairs, tables and couches for the local people. *Mark 6. 3.*

CART. In the Old Testament times wooden carts with heavy solid, or spoked, wheels drawn by oxen were the regular carriers. The flat wooden floor of the cart could be easily piled high with farm produce at harvest time. A special cart was

made to carry the Ark of the Covenant as related in the Book of Samuel.
1 Samuel 6. 7–14.

CENTURION (see also *Caesarea*). In the Roman army a thousand men were divided into ten sections of one hundred each, ten 'centuries' led by a 'centurion'. One Christian centurion, Cornelius, is named in the New Testament. In his home at Caesarea, Cornelius and his family were always ready to help their fellow Christians. God spoke to him to send messengers down the coast to Joppa to bring the apostle Peter to

Caesarea. When Peter came he found Cornelius' house full of people of different races he had not met before. Cornelius was a Roman and Peter a Jew and both learned the great truth in Caesarea that the Christian faith was for all nations, a truth which Peter recognized by baptizing all those in the house of Cornelius. *Acts 10.*

CHARIOT. 'Go up and join this chariot.' This was a surprising instruction to the apostle Philip as he watched the chariot coming near to him on the desert road. Only important men rode in chariots by themselves. The chariot swayed to a stop, and Philip saw that the man was reading a scroll. He got up beside him in the chariot and found that he was the treasurer of the Queen of Ethiopia on his way home from Jerusalem, and he was reading a piece of Isaiah's prophecy. The chariot rolled on while Philip told the man more about Jesus. So convinced was he of the truth that he ordered the chariot to stop by a pool of water and there Philip baptized him. Chariots and their horses were signs of

power and authority in Bible times. They were used in war, and in great processions, and the charioteer was always a skilled driver. *Acts 8. 26–39.*

CHERUBIM. Heavenly beings, usually with wings and human faces and thought to be very close to God. The Cherubim guarded the Tree of Life in the Garden of Eden, and also the Ark of the Lord—the most holy possession of the people of Israel.
Ezekiel 10.

CHRISTIAN (see also *Antioch*). The word *Christian* occurs three times in the New Testament which shows that it was sometimes used as a name for those who belonged to Christ's 'party', or the 'household' of Christ. Perhaps it was just a nickname, but a suitable one for those who followed Christ. *Acts 11. 26; 26. 28; 1 Peter 4. 16.*

CHRONICLES, BOOKS OF. The two Books of Chronicles in the Old Testament record the history of Israel chiefly from King David to the Captivity in Babylon. The 'Chronicler' is very interested in David and Solomon; the worship of the Temple; and in the kings who obeyed God's law.
First and Second Chronicles.

CHURCH. The word *church* in the New Testament generally means a local group, or congregation of Christians, and never a building. There were many of these 'churches' but they all believed they belonged to 'one church'. The first church in Jerusalem was made up chiefly of Christ's Jewish followers. Then came the churches in the non-Jewish world which arose out of the missionary work of the apostles. The New Testament tells us very little about the 'inside' life of these churches. But the one great truth they held in common was the confession that Jesus of Nazareth was 'Lord and Christ'—and that gave them their sense of unity. They belonged to him and were members of his Church. *Acts 9. 31; Ephesians 4.*

CIRCUMCISION. The physical act of circumcision was a sign to the men of Israel of their 'covenant' with God. It marked their obedience to God's law. In the New Testament Paul said that the important thing was the relationship it symbolized. *Genesis 17. 9–14; Galatians 5. 1–12.*

CITIES OF REFUGE. When a man in ancient Israel purposely took the life of another the duty of punishing him was the responsibility of the nearest male relative. He had the right to kill in return. But in order to protect men who killed someone accidentally six 'cities of refuge' were established. If a man could get to one of them he was safe for the time being. *Numbers 35. 9–15.*

COLOSSIANS, EPISTLE TO THE. The Christians who lived in the city of Colossae—now a ruined site in Turkey—were a small, isolated mixed group of Jews, Greeks and Asians. Many strange ideas were discussed amongst them which were not really Christian ideas at all. The Jews amongst them too were over-eager about observing their old ways of worship. Paul, away in his Rome prison, heard about this from his friend Epaphras and in the year A.D. 61 he wrote them a letter called *the Epistle to the Colossians.* The only thing for the Christians to do, he said, is to keep on loving Christ, and to get rid of everything that worked against doing Christ's will. The Colossians thought they were very wise and clever men but true wisdom, Paul wrote, comes from God. *Epistle to the Colossians.*

COMMUNION (see also *Lord's Supper*). This is a New Testament word which means 'sharing in something'. So it can also mean 'having a share', 'giving a share', or simply 'sharing'. It is a word that is linked most closely with what happened at the 'sharing' of the meal between Christ and his disciples which we call the Lord's Supper. *Luke 22. 14–23; Romans 15. 26; 2 Corinthians 9. 13.*

CONFESSION. 'Repent, for the Kingdom of Heaven is at hand.' That was the cry of John the Baptist as he preached in the wilderness of Judaea to announce the coming of Christ. He called on the people to *confess* their sins and ask God's forgiveness. That is one kind of confession. Another is the open 'confession', or 'testimony', to a personal faith in Jesus Christ. Jesus himself made this kind of confession when Pontius Pilate asked him whether he was the Christ. *Matthew 3. 1–6; 1 Timothy 6. 11–14.*

CONVERSION. 'Who are you Lord?' The cry came from Saul of Tarsus on the road to Damascus. Saul was blinded by a light from heaven and a voice spoke, 'Saul, Saul, why do you persecute me?' Saul was at his great turning point. He was 'turning to God' which is the meaning of 'conversion'. Not all believers, in the New Testament, were converted in such a dramatic way, but all were turned to God by faith in Christ. *Acts 9. 1–9.*

CORINTHIANS, EPISTLES TO THE. The famous sea-port of Corinth in Greece was

a lively, prosperous, but evil place when Paul lived in it in the year A.D. 51. The Corinthians were known for their free and easy manner of living, and the Corinthian Christians often followed the same pattern. Many Christians in Corinth forgot that they were really 'Christ's men'. Paul wrote them two long letters of advice and counsel called *Epistles to the Corinthians*. In the letters he pointed out their many faults and sympathized with them in living in a city like Corinth. But he pleaded with them to give Christ the supreme place in their hearts. That was the only way for Corinthians to be Christians. The two letters contain some of Paul's finest writing—his idea of Christian love; his teaching on the Lord's Supper; his view of the Christian ministry, and his belief in Christ's triumphant victory over death. *Epistles to the Corinthians*.

COURTS. 'Enter his gates with thanksgiving and his courts with praise.' The Psalms in the Old Testament often refer to the 'courts of the Lord', the spacious enclosures surrounding the Temple which had four courts—for the Gentiles, the Women, the Men, and the Priests. It was in the 'courts' that people assembled before worship in the Temple. The 'courts' of God's house were for his people to use and respect. *Psalms 84, 92, 96, 100, 135.*

Be Christians as well as Corinthians! That was the message Paul wrote to the 'Church of God' in Corinth

COVENANT. This is one of the most important words of the Bible. It is the word used for God's 'promise' to Israel to be their God, and on Israel's side to be his people. It signifies the special relationship between God and Israel. From the time of Abraham onwards, this 'covenant' is always being renewed by God, and it powerfully shaped the life of Israel. In the New Testament Jesus is the fulfilment of the covenant. He is the 'New Covenant'. The Church becomes the new Israel linked by covenant to God. The new covenant is even closer than the old through the life and work of Jesus. *Genesis 17. 7; Hebrews 8. 6–13.*

CRETE. A mountainous island in the Mediterranean. Crete comes into the New Testament story through Paul. His ship sailing for Rome was driven by the winds to Crete. Paul would have liked to stay there for the winter in the safety of the island's harbour but his advice was not taken and the ship was soon wrecked on the island of Malta. *Acts 27. 1–26.*

CRISPUS. Crispus belongs to that select group of people mentioned in the New Testament who turned from the Jewish to the Christian way. He was a 'leader' or a 'ruler' of the synagogue in Corinth. But on hearing Paul preach he and all his family believed and were baptized. *Acts 18. 5–11.*

CROSS. In the New Testament a 'cross' is the upright stake with a cross-beam on which criminals were hanged, or nailed, to die. Jesus himself died in that way. So the word 'cross' has come to have another and more wonderful meaning. It stands for God's love to all men which Jesus showed on the 'cross', and so has become the symbol of the Christian faith. *1 Corinthians 1. 18–25.*

CRUCIFIXION. The cruel death of crucifixion was practised by the Romans and was usually only inflicted on slaves, or the lowest type of criminal. The feet and hands of the victim were nailed to an upright cross, and he was left to die a painful and lingering death. *Luke 23. 33.*

CRUSE. 'I have only a little oil in a cruse.' The cry of the lonely widow in the midst of the famine-stricken land touched Elijah's heart. She was ready to share with him her last bit of bread and her last drop of oil so precious to a housewife for cooking. The cruse was a little pot, or jug, used for keeping oil or honey. Elijah promised her that if she baked a cake for him her supply of meal and oil would never give out. *1 Kings 17. 8–16.*

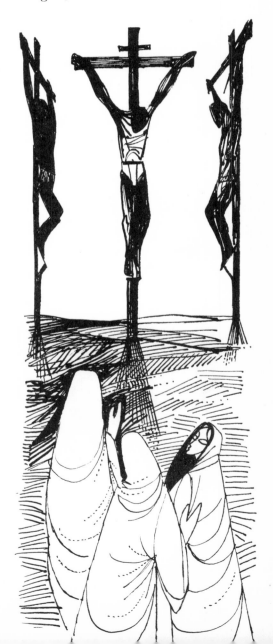

CUBIT. 'Which of you by taking thought can add one cubit to his stature?' asked Jesus of his disciples. One version of the New Testament puts it this way, 'Is there a man of you who can add a foot to his height?' A cubit was usually reckoned as the distance from elbow to finger tips, and was sometimes exactly stated as seventeen inches. Whatever the measurement only God could provide it. That was the point Jesus was making. *Matthew 6. 27.*

CYPRUS. 'You enemy of truth, you son of the devil.' These stern words were spoken by Paul on the island of Cyprus to a magician who opposed his preaching. Paul had with him Barnabas, a native of Cyprus, and the two men won a good hearing—except from this clever magician who thought he had defeated the Christian preachers. Calling on God for help Paul smote the magician with temporary blindness and the people of Cyprus marvelled at his power. Cyprus is a big island, 140 miles long by 60 wide, in the Mediterranean Sea. *Acts 13. 4–12.*

CYRENE. As Jesus struggled to carry his cross on the way to the place of crucifixion, the centurion in charge saw that it was too heavy for him. Looking around for someone to carry the heavy wooden stake, he saw a dark face in the crowd—the face of a foreigner. He ordered him to carry the cross, and the Gospels record the name of this African—a visitor to Jerusalem—as Simon from Cyrene, a port on the north coast of Africa. *Mark 15. 21–25.*

D **DAGON** (see also *Samson*). 'Our god has given Samson our enemy into our hands.' That was the cry of the Philistines when they captured the strong man of Israel. To thank their idol Dagon the Philistines planned a great feast in the god's honour. The blind Samson was brought to entertain the company. To display his wonderful strength he leaned his weight against the pillars of the house. Down they came bringing the roof with them and crushing everybody sitting beneath. *Judges 16. 23–30.*

cubit

DAMASCUS. Paul made the long journey from Jerusalem to Damascus, the capital of Syria, to persecute the Christians there. But on the way, God spoke to him so instead of condemning the Damascus Christians he preached their faith in the Jewish synagogue. Jewish merchants, since Old Testament times, liked living in Damascus with its pleasant gardens and orchards. The camel

Over the wall at Damascus! Paul
escaped by night in a basket.
Saved by his friends, he outwitted
his enemies

trade caravans brought them much business. Paul lived in a house in Straight Street and he escaped the angry Jews by being let down over the city wall in a basket. *Acts 9. 10–25.*

DAN (see also *Beersheba*) One of the twelve tribes of Israel who moved northward and settled near the source of the River Jordan. The city of Dan was the most northerly in Israel and seemed a long way from Beersheba in the south. *Judges 20. 1.*

DANIEL, BOOK OF. In the year 598 B.C. Nebuchadnezzar, king of Babylon, besieged Jerusalem. Daniel was amongst the young Jews carried off to Babylon, where he became a favourite with the king. 'Stories' about Daniel make up the book. They are 'dreams', 'messages', 'prophecies' which gave hope to the Jews and pointed forward to a 'golden age' to come. Some scholars believe the 'prophecies' of Daniel even foretell the first and second comings of Christ. *Book of Daniel.*

DAVID (see also *Anointing*). 'Arise, anoint him, for this is he.' These words were spoken by God to the prophet Samuel as he stood in the farmyard of Jesse the Bethlehemite. He had come in search of a king amongst Jesse's sons, and he chose the youngest, David, the shepherd boy. Handsome and brave, young David pleased King Saul with his music, slew Goliath the Philistine giant with his sling, and became a close friend of the king's son Jonathan. Then Saul became jealous of David's popularity and war broke out between them. After Saul's death David became king of the united kingdom of Judah and Israel and reigned in Jerusalem for thirty-three years. He made Jerusalem a prosperous city and gave the Jewish people a proud place amongst the nations. A wise king, a brave soldier, a musician and poet, David appeared to the Jews an admirable and ideal person. He also did many things that were wrong in God's sight. He was very human and yet a great king and worthy to belong to the family from which the Messiah—Jesus Christ—himself is descended. *1 Samuel 16; 2 Samuel 5. 1–10.*

DAY OF THE LORD. This phrase often occurs in the Old Testament. Many of the people imagined it would be a day of rejoicing when Israel would triumph over her enemies. But the prophets in the Old Testament said 'the day' would be a judgment day for all the public and private sins of Israel. They warned the people of what would happen on 'the day' if they disobeyed God's laws. In the New Testament the phrase often refers to the expected second coming of Christ to the earth. *Amos 5. 18–20; 1 Corinthians 1. 8.*

DEACON. In the early days of the Christian church in Jerusalem the apostles were busy men. They had to see to the organization and affairs of the young church as well as to preach and baptize. It was too much for them. So seven men of 'honest report' were chosen by the church and appointed as 'deacons' to assist them. They looked after the organization, the money and the care of the poor. The name 'deacon' comes from a Greek word *diakonos* which means 'servant' or 'table waiter'. Ever since that time the 'diaconate' has been an honourable office in the Christian church. *Acts 6. 1–6.*

DEAD SEA. In the deep rift that runs down through the Jordan Valley in Palestine lies the Dead Sea, or the Salt Sea. The great lake lies 1280 feet below sea-level and is 48 miles long and 8 miles wide. Although the Jordan and other rivers pour into it, its temperature is so high that the heat evaporates the in-coming fresh water. The Dead Sea is a vast deposit of salt and other chemicals and no fish can live in it, and anyone who swims in it just floats on the surface. *Deuteronomy 3. 17; Joshua 3. 16.*

DEAD SEA SCROLLS.—see *Scroll.*

DEBORAH. Over a thousand years before Jesus Christ there lived in the land of Israel a celebrated woman named Deborah, famous as a 'judge' and 'prophetess'. The Israelites listened to her advice and respected her wisdom. In the war against the Canaanites, under their general Sisera, Deborah encouraged the Israelite army until Sisera was defeated. Her famous 'song of deliverance' is one of the great chapters in the Book of Judges. *Judges 5.*

DEBTS (see also *Forgiveness*). 'Forgive us our debts, as we also have forgiven our debtors.' The phrase that Jesus used in the Lord's Prayer is a link with the old Jewish practice of granting a loan to a friend. If he was in difficulty about repaying it he was not pressed to repay the loan. Jesus was not concerned about loans and debts of money but with the 'forgiving spirit'. His prayer was for the forgiving spirit always and in all things. *Matthew 6. 7–15.*

DECAPOLIS. News about Jesus spread all round the shores of the Sea of Galilee even to the towns of Decapolis which were mostly to the south-east of the lake. There

'No hurt was found upon Daniel because he had trusted in his God' (p. 25)

Jesus met an unhappy man suffering from mental illness who terrified the local people with his outbursts of madness. He calmed down on meeting Jesus. 'Come out of the man, you unclean spirits,' said Jesus, and the 'spirits' ran into a herd of pigs which raced in mad fury down the hill and were drowned in the lake. Decapolis is a Greek word meaning 'ten cities' and this region probably had more Gentiles than Jews. The cured madman went calmly amongst the people describing what Jesus had done for him. *Mark 5. 1–20.*

DECREE. A word used in the Bible to indicate a 'proclamation', 'announcement' or legal decision. Luke records the 'decree' of the Roman Emperor to hold a census which brought Joseph and Mary to Bethlehem. *Luke 2. 1.*

DELILAH (see also *Samson*). When the Philistines were trying to capture Samson, the strong man of Israel, they persuaded Delilah to discover from Samson the secret of his strength. His strength came, she found, from his uncut hair. Delilah betrayed his secret. Samson's hair was cut as he slept and in his weakness he was blinded and led away into captivity by the Philistines. *Judges 16. 15–22.*

DEMAS. In his letters Paul often mentions the names of his friends and Demas was one of them. He calls him 'my fellow worker', and then later he sadly records, 'Demas has deserted me'. Perhaps Demas was homesick for his own home at Salonika and tired of travelling with the restless apostle. *Philemon v. 23; 2 Timothy 4. 10.*

DEMETRIUS. There was uproar in the city of Ephesus amongst the silversmiths, the craftsmen who produced the beautiful little statues of the goddess Diana. They said that their craft was in danger. All because of the preaching of the apostle Paul who dared to say that gods made with human hands were not gods at all. Demetrius was a leader of the silversmiths, and led them to the city centre shouting 'Great is Diana of the Ephesians', and the city mob joined in the shouting. The Town Clerk was brought out to speak to the crowd and he warned Demetrius that if he and his friends had a complaint against anyone, they should make it through the courts of law. Paul wisely stayed at home and soon afterwards left the city. *Acts 19. 23–41.*

DEMON.—see *Devil.*

DENARIUS. 'Whose is this image and superscription?' asked Jesus as he held the *denarius,* the 'penny', in his hand. He looked at the coin and saw that the figure engraved there was the Roman Emperor's. The *denarius* was a common silver coin of the day worth about 17 cents U.S.A. and 1s. 3d. British. It was the pay of a labourer for a

'Delilah called a man and had him shave off the seven locks of Samson's head'

day's work. When the Good Samaritan paid the innkeeper to look after the robbed man, he gave him two pennies, two *denarii* —a generous payment.
Matthew 22. 19; Luke 10. 35.

DERBE. A city of Asia Minor, now in Turkey, visited by Paul and Barnabas on their missionary journey. One of Paul's helpers, Gaius, came from Derbe. The Christian church there must have been a fairly strong one. *Acts 14. 6.*

DESERT. The Bible uses the words 'desert' and 'wilderness' to describe open country of sand dunes, scrubby pasture lands, and barren rocky places. The people of Israel in their wanderings from Egypt to the Promised Land spent long years crossing this sort of country. It was not all sand, or without water and green grass, but it was generally dry, hot and barren. *Exodus 5. 3; Deuteronomy 32. 10.*

the book describes how Moses went up to the top of Mount Pisgah to look over the Promised Land—the land to which he led the people but never entered.
Book of Deuteronomy.

DEVIL. The word 'devil' or 'demon' often occurs in the Gospels and refers to a 'being' hostile to God and men. Jesus met people possessed of the 'devil' who cried out against him and the good he was doing. They were not just 'sick' or 'mad' but 'devil possessed'. Only Jesus was able to triumph over the 'devil' in them.
Matthew 8. 28–32; Luke 11. 14–20.

DIANA (see also *Demetrius*). Another name for Artemis, the goddess of the Ephesians. Her temple at Ephesus was one of the wonders of the world. The silversmiths of Ephesus made silver models of the temple and did a big trade with pilgrims to Ephesus. They were afraid that the coming of the

The Roman silver 'penny' (p. 27)

'Great is Diana of the Ephesians! Our trade is in danger! Let's get rid of this man Paul' (p. 27)

DEUTERONOMY, BOOK OF. Fifth book in the order of the books in the Bible. The word means 'repetition of the law'. It was always highly valued by the Jews as their book of law. In it the writer traces some of the journeys of the people of Israel and then describes how Moses received the Decalogue, or Ten Commandments. After that come detailed instructions for the conduct of daily life. These instructions show what are the blessings of obedience and the penalties of disobedience to the laws and regulations of Jewish life. In the last chapter

Christian faith to their city might take away their living. *Acts 19. 28.*

Daughter of Jupiter and twin sister of Apollo, Diana was the goddess of hunting. Her temple at Ephesus had a hundred massive columns: the silversmiths sold models of it

DIDYMUS. This is the Greek 'surname' of the apostle Thomas and means 'the twin'. John uses the name three times but does not mention who the 'twin' is. *John 11. 16.*

DINAH. When Jacob camped near the city of Shechem his daughter Dinah called on the local womenfolk. There she met the young prince of Shechem who fell in love with her. He was so eager to make Dinah his wife that he was ready to observe all the Hebrew customs required of him by Jacob and his family. But Dinah's brothers were so angered by the attitude of the young prince towards their sister that they killed him and his father Hamor. *Genesis 34.*

29

'Come follow me'

DIONYSIUS THE AREOPAGITE. 'Men of Athens, I perceive that in every way you are very religious.' That was Paul's opening sentence in his address to the members of the learned council called the Areopagus in Athens. All of them were interested in religious questions, for it was part of their duty to watch over the moods and manners of the citizens. One member, Dionysius, listened eagerly to Paul's preaching and believed what he said. But most of the Areopagites laughed at Paul's strange teaching. 'We will hear you again,' they said. But Dionysius spoke to Paul and joined him. *Acts 17. 22–34.*

DISCIPLE. When Jesus called his 'disciples' he described them as 'learners' or 'pupils' because that is what the word means. He gave them 'power'; he 'sent them out'. A disciple, he said, should follow his master and his example. He must learn from him. The names of the disciples are listed in the Gospels, but Jesus never thought of them as the only ones. 'Disciples' is a name for all the followers of Jesus anywhere and at any time. *Matthew 10. 1–25.*

DISEASE. The Bible has many accounts of diseases and illnesses, and of the ways in which they were treated. Some of the diseases in the Bible are easily recognizable by modern doctors, but others like 'palsy', 'fever', 'issue' are rather vague in their meaning. The Bible mentions diseases of the mind as well as the body. In the Old Testament Book of Leviticus the Jews were given many detailed instructions about health and hygiene in order to prevent disease. In the New Testament Jesus showed in his healing miracles the importance of faith in the healing of disease. *Deuteronomy 28. 27–28; Luke 4. 40–41; Acts 14. 8–10.*

DISPERSION. 'Now there were dwelling in Jerusalem Jews, devout men from every nation under heaven.' That sentence from the Acts of the Apostles shows how the Jewish people had spread, or dispersed, all round the world. In the same chapter there is a long list of the countries they came from, all speaking different languages but all of them Jews. Wherever the Jews went for trade and business, they established synagogues for the worship of God, and when the first apostles began to travel they nearly always preached in the synagogues. Most of the 'dispersed' Jews did not believe the new faith but some of them did. *Acts 2. 5–13.*

DOG. In the lands of the Bible the dog is usually the scavenger, the animal who helps to get rid of the rubbish. There is one little picture of a dog in the Gospels. When Jesus was talking to the Canaanite woman who asked him to help her, he tested her faith by asking whether the children's bread should be thrown to the dogs. She saw the point. She herself was but a 'dog' in the eyes of the Jews, only fit to have what was left. But she said that at home even the little dogs that lay under the table were allowed to eat the crumbs. Jesus respected the woman's ready answer and her faith, and he healed her daughter.
Matthew 15. 21–28.

DORCAS. 'She was full of good works and acts of charity.' The name of Dorcas has always been treasured in the Christian story because Dorcas of Joppa was such a person. She is the only woman to be named a *disciple* in the New Testament. A capable needlewoman, a good dressmaker and a practical person in every way, Dorcas was at the heart of the church in Joppa. When she died the church there sent an urgent message to the apostle Peter to come. Peter prayed by the body and asked God to give Dorcas back to the church again. Peter presented her alive once more to the Joppa Christians. *Acts 9. 36–42.*

DOTHAN (see also *Elisha*). In the fighting between the kingdoms of Israel and Syria, Israel had one advantage—the advice and secret information of the prophet Elisha. Elisha lived in the city of Dothan in the fertile plain between the hills of Samaria and the hills of Carmel. The king of Syria determined to capture him and sent a great host of warriors to surround the city and seize the prophet. When Elisha's servant looked out in the early morning, he was frightened to see so great an army. 'Alas, my master,' he said, 'what shall we do?' Then Elisha prayed, and the young man looked again and this time he saw that the hill of Dothan was also full of horses and chariots surrounding Elisha. The prophet prayed again and a temporary blindness afflicted the Syrian warriors, who were led as captives to the king of Israel. When their eyes opened again Elisha advised the king to give them food and send them home unharmed to the king of Syria. That act stopped the raids of the Syrians into the land of Israel. *2 Kings 6. 11–23.*

From the hill-top of Dothan Syria's army looked terrible. But Elisha's faith in God proved more than a match for them

DOVE. A very common bird in Palestine and considered to be ceremonially clean for use in the Temple worship. Doves were sold in the courts of the Temple. When Jesus was baptized by John the Baptist in the River Jordan the Holy Spirit descended on him 'like a dove'. It was a dove that Noah sent out from the Ark to survey the Great Flood. The dove came back with an olive leaf in its beak—a sign that the waters were going down. *Genesis 8. 6–12; Mark 1. 10.*

DRAGON (see also *Satan*). 'A great red dragon, with seven heads and ten horns, and seven diadems upon his heads.' That is the picture the Book of Revelation gives of a mythical monster. It is pictorial language for 'Satan', or 'Evil One'. In the Old Testament it may be that the 'whale' or the 'crocodile' is also the 'dragon'—the monster of the sea and the land who was always lurking to destroy. Finally, in the war against the dragon in the Revelation Michael and his angels win a great victory over Evil. *Revelation 12. 1–12.*

'O that I had wings
like a dove'
(Psalm 55)

DREAMS. 'And Jacob dreamed that there was a ladder set up on the earth, and the top of it reached to heaven.' The dream of Jacob as he lay with his head on the pillow of hard stone is one of the most famous in the Bible. Out of his dream Jacob learned that his family would become a great nation. God spoke to him in his dream, and when he awoke he said, 'Surely the Lord is in this place, and I did not know it.' The Bible records two sorts of dreams. There were those dreams of the prophets, like

Dulcimer.
Forerunner of
the bagpipe?

that of Jacob, which had messages from God in them. There were others, like those of Pharaoh and Nebuchadnezzar, which described possible happenings in the future. *Genesis 28. 10–17; 41. 14–36.*

DRUSILLA. Wife of Felix the Roman governor who tried Paul. She was a Jewess and tradition says that it was Drusilla more than her husband who was eager to save Paul, and often talked with him while he was in prison. *Acts 24. 24–26.*

DULCIMER. Nebuchadnezzar the king of Babylon made an image of gold. He commanded an orchestra to play and at the sound of the music all the people were to fall down and worship the great image. The king's orchestra included the dulcimer, which is supposed to have been rather like a bagpipe. *Daniel 3.*

DUMB. 'Master, I brought my son to you, for he has a dumb spirit.' Jesus responded to that cry from the heart of a father. The boy could not speak and was deaf as well, and had fits which threw him into convulsions. Jesus commanded the 'spirit' to come out of the boy and when he fell to the ground, prostrate and rigid, Jesus took him by the hand and lifted him up quite well again. Dumbness is mentioned twenty-four times in the Bible. The ways of curing it practised today were not known, and the dumb were more pitied than helped. *Mark 9. 14–29.*

E EAR. 'Hear, O heavens, and give ear, O earth.' In these words Isaiah the prophet opens his prophecy. He uses the expressive word 'ear' which the Bible often uses. In this sense it means to listen, take notice. It also means the physical 'ear' or an 'ear' of barley, or corn. When Jesus wished to emphasize his talk to his listeners he used the phrase 'He who has ears to hear, let him hear.' *Matthew 11. 15.*

EARNEST. A word used by trading merchants and adopted by Paul in his letters. It means the 'deposit' on the purchase price, a 'guarantee' that the rest will follow. For Paul the gift of Holy Spirit is an 'earnest' of all the glory that will follow for the Christian. *Ephesians 1. 14.*

EAR-RINGS. In the third chapter of Isaiah there is a list of the ornaments worn by Hebrew women and ear-rings is amongst them. The prophet was not against ornaments of this kind but he warned about being too proud of them. *Isaiah 3. 16–26.*

Ear-rings went with a fine dress

EARTHQUAKE. 'And the earth did quake and the rocks rent.' That is how Matthew describes the earthquake at the time of the crucifixion of Jesus Christ. There are many other instances in the Bible of the earth moving and shaking: the layers of rock which make up the land of Palestine often shift their position and cause a 'quake'. *Zechariah 14. 1–11; Matthew 27. 51–53.*

Trading in 'earnest'! It guaranteed the full payment

EBED-MELECH. When Jeremiah, the prophet, was imprisoned in the dreadful dungeon during the siege of Jerusalem, one man had pity on him. He was Ebed-Melech, a servant of King Zedekiah. He knew that in the mud and filth of the deep dungeon there was no water and no food. Jeremiah would soon die. He went to the king and pleaded that he should be allowed to get the prophet out of the pit, and the king gave him permission. So Ebed-Melech collected some strong men and a supply of long ropes. He threw down the pit pieces of old cloth and shouted to Jeremiah to put them under his arms so that the ropes would not cut into him. Then they hauled him up. *Jeremiah 38. 6–13.*

EBENEZER. In the fighting between the Israelites and the Philistines the prophet Samuel prayed to God for Israel's victory. He went with the warriors encouraging them and offering prayers as the battle went on. When the Philistines were defeated Samuel set up a little monument of remembrance and thanksgiving—and called it 'Ebenezer', which means 'stone of help'. *1 Samuel 7. 7–12.*

ECCLESIASTES. Sometimes this book, in the Old Testament, is known as 'the Preacher' or 'the Teacher'. In it the writer is searching for the meaning of life. He sees it like a riddle and tries to find the answer to the puzzle. He comes to the conclusion

that it is God who holds the key to the mysteries of living and that man must trust God. Life is given to men day by day, and the things of everyday are the ones through which men can glorify God. Many of the things which people like to have—money, pleasure, fame and possessions—are not the real treasures of life. That is to be found only in knowing about God and serving him. *Ecclesiastes*.

EDEN, GARDEN OF. 'And the Lord God planted a garden eastward in Eden.' It was a beautiful, well ordered, and well planted garden fit for the first man, Adam, to live in. The Book of Genesis relates this great story of harmony and of an ideal existence at the beginning of the world. There Adam and his wife, Eve, were obedient to God's commands—until sin entered their hearts and spoiled their relationship with God. They were tempted by the serpent to eat the forbidden fruit. They fell to the tempter. They had to leave the lovely garden where they had been happy in the companionship of God. Their disobedience to God brought them hardship, suffering and unhappiness, but God did not forsake them. The Book of Genesis describes Eden as in the region of the Euphrates and Tigris rivers. *Genesis 2 and 3*.

EDOM (see also *Esau*). 'And Esau said to Jacob, Feed me, I pray thee, with some of that red pottage; for I am faint; therefore was his name called Edom.' Under the name

'Every tree that is pleasant and good for food'

of Edom, which means red, Esau's descendants, known as Edomites, lived in the land south of the Dead Sea stretching towards the Red Sea. It is a rugged area of red stone. The Edomites regularly defended their patches of farmland against attacks from the Israel side of Jordan. Edomites and Israelites were ancient rivals. *Genesis 25. 30–34.*

EGYPT. The names Egypt and Egyptians are mentioned over two hundred times in the Bible. The rich black soil of the valley of the Nile, in the north of Africa, was a wonderful food provider, and that gave Egypt great importance. All the people of the Bible knew about Egypt and its powerful Pharaoh - Kings, its buildings and its civilization. It was in Egypt that Moses called the people of Israel to be 'the people of God', and from there they began the wanderings that led them to the Promised Land. Egypt had many bad memories for the Israelites, and their prophets often reminded them of the wonderful goodness of God in leading them out of their Egyptian captivity. Egypt was the land of their slavery but also the land where God gave them their freedom—a land to hate but also a memory to love. *Exodus 1–14.*

EHUD. The only left-handed man mentioned by name in the Bible. In the revolt of Israel against Moab, Ehud planned to kill Eglon, king of Moab, who was very fat and slow in his movements. Ehud brought him a present and asked to speak with him alone. It was a hot day and the king sat by himself in his summer house to talk with his visitor. Ehud's dagger was on his right thigh underneath his cloak. But he struck with his left hand—a trick that deceived and killed the king. *Judges 3. 14–22.*

Egypt - land of plenty

EKRON. One of the five main towns of the Philistines which fell into the hands of the Hebrew invaders but was fought over many times afterwards. Ekron was famous for its god Baal-Zebub which may be the Beelzebub mentioned in the Gospels. *2 Kings 1. 1–16.*

ELAH. Just eleven miles south-west of Jerusalem is the valley of Elah called today Wadi es-Samt—a favourite way of approaching the city. It was much used by the Philistines in their wars with Israel, and in this valley David won his victory over Goliath. *1 Samuel 17. 2.*

ELAMITES. Amongst the foreign peoples listed in the Acts of the Apostles on the day of Pentecost are the Elamites. They came from the country of Elam at the head of the Persian Gulf, where the River Tigris enters the sea. *Acts 2. 9.*

ELATH. As the children of Israel wandered northwards from Egypt to the Promised Land they had many stopping places where there was water and shady palm trees. One of them was Elath on the sea of the Gulf of Aqabah—an offshoot of the Red Sea. In later years King Solomon kept his ships at Elath, sending them out to collect gold and precious stones from the Red Sea ports to enrich the palace and temple in Jerusalem. *Deuteronomy 2. 8; 1 Kings 9. 26.*

ELEAZAR. The third son of Aaron who succeeded his father in the priestly office to the people of Israel during their journey to the Promised Land. *Deuteronomy 10. 6.*

ELI (see also *Hannah, Samuel*). Eli was priest in the Shiloh Temple for forty years from about the year 1115 B.C. He was there in the days when Hannah the mother of Samuel brought her little son to dedicate him to the work of the Temple. Eli's own sons, who might have succeeded him as priests, were not fit to do so. Eli was glad to 'adopt' Samuel to help him in the

Temple. When the old man became blind it was Samuel who led him about, and when God spoke to Eli it was through the sensitive mind of the young boy. It was Eli's supreme duty to guard the sacred Ark, and when in battle the Philistines captured the Ark Eli was so shocked that he fell off his seat and died as a result of the fall.
1 Samuel 1–4.

ELIAB. When the prophet Samuel came down to the farm of Jesse the Bethlehemite to choose a leader for the people from Jesse's sons he was introduced to Eliab. This handsome, tall young man, the eldest of the eight sons, looked like a real possibility. But he, like all the others, was passed over in favour of David. There are a dozen and more Eliabs in the Old Testament.
1 Samuel 16. 6.

Egypt - land of vast buildings such as the pyramids built by slave labour

Egypt - land of the River Nile, once the home of a rich civilization whose wonders still startle us

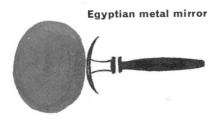

Egyptian metal mirror

'The prophets of Baal called upon Baal from morning until noon, but no one answered.' (Elijah remembered his ravens and trusted in God)

ELIAKIM. When the Assyrians were threatening Jerusalem in the days of King Hezekiah in 701 B.C., Eliakim was in charge of his household. Sennacherib the Assyrian king sent his ambassador Rabshakeh to the city. To meet him Hezekiah sent Eliakim. Rabshakeh appealed to Eliakim and the people to throw in their lot with the great empire of Assyria. Eliakim listened patiently to his mocking speech and reported to the king and to the prophet Isaiah. Eliakim's watchfulness rallied the nation against the Assyrian threat. Eliakim is a common name in the Old Testament and means 'God establishes'. *2 Kings 18–19.*

ELIEZER. David brought the Ark of God into Jerusalem with much rejoicing and ceremony. Seven priests sounded the trumpets and one of them was named Eliezer which means 'God is my help'. The second son of Moses was also called Eliezer and when Luke in his Gospel lists the forebears of Jesus he includes the name Eliezer. *1 Chronicles 15. 24.*

ELIHU. One of the friends of Job who spoke to him sincerely and frankly. Elihu was afraid to speak at first because he was the youngest of Job's friends. 'Great men,' he said to Job, 'are not always wise; neither do the aged understand judgment.' He interpreted for Job in his suffering the ways of God. *Job 32.*

ELIJAH (see also *Ahab*). Nine hundred years before Jesus, the prophet Elijah came into the land of Israel. It was at a time of famine and drought and Elijah went hungry and thirsty like everyone else. In the country area where he lived there was no food but every day God provided Elijah with food brought to him by the ravens and he drank water from the trickle in the brook. This proved to Elijah that God would care for him. He preached the greatness and authority of the one true God. He had a long struggle to convince the people of Israel of these truths. They ran after other gods (*baal*). To put the issue to the test Elijah with the prophets of the *baal* called a great assembly on Mount Carmel. Elijah challenged the priests of the gods to pray for fire to come down to burn the bullocks on the sacrificial altar. All day they prayed but nothing happened. Then Elijah prepared his sacrifice, soaked it in water, and prayed for fire. The flames descended and burnt up the sacrifice. All the people fell on their knees and shouted 'The Lord he is the God.'
1 Kings 18. 17–39.

ELIM. The second stopping place of the Israelites after they had crossed the Red Sea—just east of the modern Suez Canal. *Exodus 15. 27.*

ELISHA (see also *Dothan* and *Naaman*). 'And Elijah passed by him, and cast his mantle upon him, and he left his oxen and ran after Elijah.' In this dramatic way Elijah chose his successor Elisha who for more than fifty years was a prophet in Israel. He moved amongst the simple peasant people, lived in kings' houses, advised on affairs of state and, like Elijah, was always reminding the people of their duty to God. One of the finest stories about him is the one in which the woman of Shunem and her husband prepared him a little room in their house. With a bed, a table, a chair and a lamp, Elisha used the room whenever he wished. When the woman's son died Elisha raised him from the dead. His fame spread through all the land of Israel and far beyond it as a man of God who not only preached about God but used the very powers of God. *2 Kings 4. 8–37.*

ELIZABETH. 'Blessed art thou among women.' That was the greeting of Elizabeth to her cousin Mary, before Jesus was born. Elizabeth was the wife of Zechariah and knew the wonderful secret of the coming of Jesus. It was her own son John the Baptist who publicly preached the good news of Christ's appearance. *Luke 1. 42.*

ELOI, ELOI, LAMA SABACHTHANI. As Jesus was nearing the end of his agony on the Cross he cried in a loud voice—'My God, my God, why hast thou forsaken me?' Jesus remembered the phrase from Psalm 22, which tells how God answers man's cry in need. Jesus spoke the words in the Aramaic language of his daily conversation, which shows how deeply personal the cry was. *Mark 15. 34–37.*

EMMAUS. Two disciples of Jesus were walking on the road to Emmaus, a village about seven miles from Jerusalem. They were talking eagerly about what happened in the city at the Crucifixion and Resurrection of Jesus. Suddenly a stranger joined them and walked and talked with them. They were surprised he seemed not to know much about the events in Jerusalem, but by the way he talked there seemed to be something unusual about him. In the village they all stopped to eat. And then the stranger took bread and blessed it and handed it round. Then they saw it was Jesus himself.

He vanished from Emmaus and the two men hurried back to Jerusalem to tell his disciples that they had seen the Lord. *Luke 24. 13–35.*

ENDOR. When King Saul misguidedly wished to peer into the future, he disguised himself and went by night to consult the witch who lived in Endor, a town in the north of Palestine. The anxious, frightened king sat before the witch. What secrets could she tell him? She made the spirit of Samuel the prophet appear to him, who told Saul of the doom waiting for him in the coming battle with the Philistines. Saul fell on his face in misery and would not eat until at last the witch persuaded him and his servants to eat the tasty meal she provided. *1 Samuel 28. 7–25.*

ENOCH. Only two men in the Bible are described as having 'walked with God'. One is Noah and the other Enoch. And Enoch shares with Elijah the distinction of being taken into the presence of God without dying. The Bible says he lived for 365 years, and the Hebrews looked on Enoch as a holy and devout man who learned many secrets about God. He was the father of Methuselah who lived for 969 years— the oldest man in all the world. *Genesis 5. 24.*

EPAPHRAS. A keen, active missionary of the early church associated with Paul who calls him his 'fellow-slave' and 'fellow-prisoner'. He visited Paul in prison in Rome and kept him in touch with the affairs of the churches. It was through his report on the church in Colossae that Paul wrote his letter to the Colossians. *Colossians 4. 12.*

EPAPHRODITUS. A messenger of the church of Philippi to Paul in prison in Rome. It was a long and tiring journey and Epaphroditus became seriously ill. Paul was grateful to the thoughtful Philippians and says that what Epaphroditus did was a 'fragrant offering'. *Philippians 4. 14–20.*

EPHAH. An ephah was a vessel big enough for a person to sit down in—a kind of bath—and used to measure liquids. Today it would hold over four gallons. *Zechariah 5. 5–11.*

EPHESIANS, EPISTLE TO THE. Paul wrote one of his greatest letters to the Christians who lived in and around the city of Ephesus. It consists of only six short

the 'body of Christ' and calls on all Christians to work together to build it up and to be worthy of belonging to it. *Epistle to the Ephesians.*

EPHESUS (see also *Demetrius*). The once great city of Ephesus is now a vast collection of ruined buildings in Turkey. In the days of Paul it was an important sea-port, the home of skilled craftsmen in silver, and the

Ephesus was a centre of civilization and culture - and also the home of a strong group of Christians amongst whom Paul lived

chapters and was probably written in prison at Rome. It is essentially a letter about 'the church', its purpose, the people in it, its relation to Christ and, above all, its unity. Paul shows that 'the church' is part of God's plan for bringing all sorts of people together in fellowship. He compares it to

centre of the worship of the goddess Artemis, or Diana. Paul lived in and around the city for two years using it as headquarters for his missionary work in the area. *Acts 19. 8–20.*

EPHOD (see also *Girdle*). The upper garment worn by Jewish priests. There were

two sorts of ephods, one of plain linen for the priests, and a more elaborate, embroidered one for the high priest done in colours of gold, blue, crimson and purple.
Leviticus 8. 7.

EPHPHATHA. This was the word Jesus spoke to the deaf man who also had a stammer in his speech. Jesus put his fingers in the man's ears, touched his tongue, and said to him, in Aramaic, 'Ephphatha' or 'be opened'. From then on the man could hear, and could speak plainly. *Mark 7. 31–35.*

EPHRAIM. Ephraim, the second son of Joseph. His descendants settled in a part of the hilly, fertile country of central Palestine. *Joshua 16. 1–10.*

EPHRATH. The ancient name of Bethlehem as used in the Old Testament.
Genesis 35. 16–21.

EPICUREANS. 'What would this babbler say?' That is what the Epicurean philosophers in Athens said about Paul. They were always ready to listen to the latest fashion in ideas, and wondered what this strange Jew had got to say. Founded by Epicurus in 306 B.C. the Epicureans were men looking and searching for happiness. They hoped to attain their goal by serenity and detachment from life, and had no belief in life after death. *Acts 17. 18–21.*

EPISTLE. A Bible word meaning 'letter'. In the Greek language it is *epistole* and in Latin *epistula*. The most famous examples in the Bible are the epistles, or letters, of Paul. An epistle was always an intimate piece of writing from one person to another, or to a group of people. *Epistles of Paul.*

ERASTUS. One of Paul's helpers. Erastus was sent with Timothy into Greece while Paul continued to work in the Ephesus area. Later he lived in Corinth.
Acts 19. 21–22.

ESAU (see also *Birthright, Edom*). The twin elder son of Isaac and Rebekah who was hairy and red from his boyhood: a great hunter who made savoury meals for his old blind father and was his father's favourite. His mother favoured his twin brother, Jacob. While Esau was off hunting Rebekah and Jacob saw their chance to trick the old man. They made a tasty dish and covered Jacob's smooth hands and neck with a hairy skin. Isaac felt the hairy hands and smelt the savoury smell, and thought that Esau had returned. So there and then he gave the crafty Jacob his fatherly blessing and all his inheritance. When Esau returned the trick was discovered, and Esau wept bitterly. The two brothers became sworn enemies and the quarrels of Esau's descendants, the Edomites, and Jacob's descendants, the Israelites, are traced to this incident, although the two brothers did become friends again. *Genesis 27. 5–41.*

ESDRAELON. Stretching from near the sea at Mount Carmel towards the Jordan Valley is the fertile plain of Esdraelon. It is watered by the River Kishon, and through it runs the important east-west road from the Jordan to the Mediterranean.
Isaiah 28. 1–4.

ESTHER, BOOK OF. Esther who became the wife of a Persian king has always been honoured by the Jewish people. Scholars have not been able to decide whether the Book of Esther is 'history' or a kind of 'novel' which shows how a group of exiled Jews lived in a Persian city about 480 B.C., and how they were saved from death by the bravery of Esther. It is a record of how God preserved his own people in a foreign land. *Book of Esther.*

ETHIOPIA (see also *Chariot*). Nowadays Ethiopia, the great country in the east of Africa, is often called Abyssinia. The Bible mentions Ethiopia and Ethiopians thirty-five times. Its people are said to be descendants of Cush, the grandson of Noah. The best known of them to Bible readers is the Ethiopian converted through Philip. Many

Ethiopians believe that this conversion ful-filled the prophecy in Psalm 68.
Psalm 68. 31; Acts 8. 26–40.

EUNICE. When Paul writes to his young friend Timothy about the Christian faith he reminds him of the example of his mother, Eunice, and his grandmother Lois. He is sure that the faith they had is continued in Timothy. Paul was a welcome visitor to Eunice's home in Lystra. *2 Timothy 1. 5.*

Isaac said 'The voice is Jacob's voice, but the hands are Esau's'

EUPHRATES. One of the great rivers of the Bible lands which rises in Turkey and flows across the vast plains of Mesopotamia for 1200 miles to empty into the Persian Gulf. Sometimes it is referred to as 'the river' or 'the great river'. Famous cities, such as Babylon, were on its banks. *Deuteronomy 11. 24; 2 Kings 24.7.*

EUTYCHUS. 'Eutychus was sitting in the window. He sank into a deep sleep as Paul talked still longer.' Was it because he did not understand the apostle? Was it because of the stuffy atmosphere? At any rate it was past midnight and this young lad of Troas was tired. In his sleep he fell three storeys and was picked up for dead. Paul took him in his arms, restored him to life, and then went on with his speech. Eutychus is a Greek name which quite appropriately means 'lucky'. *Acts 20. 7–12.*

EVANGELIST. The one who announces 'the good news' or 'preaches the Gospel'. The 'evangelist' seems to have been distinct from the office of 'apostle'. The name was also given later to the writers of the four Gospels. *Ephesians 4. 11.*

EVE. The first woman, the wife of Adam, and mother of Cain, Abel and Seth. According to the story in Genesis, Eve was made out of one of the ribs of Adam. It was Eve who ate the forbidden fruit and tempted Adam to do the same, the act which led to their banishment from the garden. *Genesis 3. 20.*

EVIL. In the Bible whatever is opposite to 'good' is 'evil'. All the way through the Bible there are many contrasts between that which is 'evil' and that which is 'good'. There is physical evil which men outwardly inflict on one another, and moral evil which results from a man's inner

'The people of Israel went up out of the land of Egypt on foot'

misdeeds. The Bible records the long warfare between good and evil in human life. God's final answer to it is in the victory of Jesus Christ over all forms of evil, and over death itself in the Resurrection.
Romans 8.

EXODUS, BOOK OF.   Exodus is the name given to the great movement of the Hebrew people out of Egypt and into the Promised Land of Palestine. The word means 'going out'. The second book in the Bible is called 'Exodus'. It contains the great story of this movement of the people, and the granting of the law by which they were to be governed. The book describes how they became a 'nation'. It happened about 1300 years before the coming of Christ and was part of the long preparation of Israel to receive God's greatest gift in Christ.
Book of Exodus.

EZEKIEL.   The prophet Ezekiel's name means 'God strengthens'. In the year 597 B.C. he was carried off, with many other Jews, to exile in Babylon. He was a young priest of twenty-five, of good family, and his message was respected by the Jews in exile. They must live, he said, by dependence on God who will one day restore his glory in the life of his own people. Ezekiel helped the exiled Jews to endure their life in a foreign land, and to prepare themselves for the future. He died in exile probably in 570 B.C.   *Ezekiel 1. 1–3.*

EZEKIEL, BOOK OF.   Ezekiel's prophecies are gathered in the book bearing his name. They are centred round the worship of God in the ideal Temple of the future which

he describes in exact detail. He shows the Jews in exile that God and the worship of God must be at the heart of their life. Only God can restore them. God's divine plan and God's law must be the pattern of their national and personal life. It is a great book of faith with truth in it for all people and nations. *Book of Ezekiel.*

EZRA. Ezra was a leader of the Jews in their captivity in Babylonia. He was adviser to the king of Persia on Jewish affairs and on the plan for the Jews to return to Jerusalem. In 458 B.C. Ezra led a large company of Jews back to the city with valuable gifts for the Temple. He was commissioned to enforce the Jewish law and to organize Jewish life once again in its old home. Later on he worked with Nehemiah in re-building the walls of Jerusalem. *Ezra 7. 1–10.*

EZRA, BOOK OF. The Book of Ezra is part of the great 'chronicle' of Jewish history. It describes how the Jews in exile in Babylon were permitted to return home. It gives the register of those who returned and of the plans made for them in Jerusalem, including the re-building schemes for the Temple. It describes Ezra's arrival and how he dealt with affairs in Jerusalem. Whether Ezra himself was the final compiler of the 'chronicle' is not certain. *Book of Ezra.*

F FAIR HAVENS. A bay on the south coast of Crete, where the ship carrying Paul called on the apostle's voyage to Rome. *Acts 27. 8.*

FAITH. 'Now faith is the assurance of things hoped for, the conviction of things not seen.' In those words the writer of the letter to the Hebrews says what faith is. It is 'trust', 'hope', 'belief' all put together in one great word. The New Testament then sums it up in the person of Jesus Christ. He is the one to have faith in. To believe in him, to have trust in him, to rely on him, is to have faith. *Hebrews 11.*

FAMINE. 'There will arise seven years of famine, and all the plenty will be forgotten in the land of Egypt; the famine will consume the land.' In these words Joseph interpreted the dream of Pharaoh and prophesied famine when the rivers would be dry and food scarce. Egypt was dependent on the River Nile overflowing its banks each year. Palestine was dependent on regular rain. When these supplies of water failed there was likely to be a food scarcity —famine. The word 'famine' is mentioned over seventy times in the Bible, which shows that the fear of famine and hunger was a very real one in Bible times. *Genesis 41. 25–57; Luke 4.25.*

FAN. The 'fan' was a long wooden 'fork' used by threshers to toss grain into the air so that the chaff could be blown away by the wind. John the Baptist used this phrase to describe God's way of separating 'good' from 'evil'. *Matthew 3. 12.*

'The land fainted by reason of the famine'

FARTHING (see also *Denarius*). A Roman copper coin (*assarion*) worth one-sixteenth of the value of a *denarius*, about 1 cent U.S.A. or 0.86 of a penny British. Matthew says two sparrows could be bought for a farthing. *Matthew 10. 29.*

FASTING. Going without food and drink for a definite period of time is looked on in the Bible as a religious act. The Jews fasted on certain days as part of their worship. They also fasted when they were sad, or when they were seeking God's particular guidance. Jesus said that 'fasting' was a useful practice as long as it was done sincerely towards God and not towards man. *Matthew 6. 16–18.*

FEAR. The word 'fear' is used scores of times in the Bible and in many different ways. In the Old Testament it usually means 'reverence' or 'respect' for God—to have 'the fear of the Lord'. The New Testament also teaches men to think of God as a 'loving' God, one who is 'father'. The two meanings taken together create a 'loving reverence' towards God. *1 John 4. 18.*

FEASTS. 'Feasts' in the Old Testament were occasions in the year when the Jews remembered the great events of their history. They were times of rejoicing and thanksgiving. There were three main feasts, or festivals—the Feast of Unleavened Bread (to remember the deliverance from Egypt); the Feast of Weeks (or Pentecost); the Feast of Tabernacles (the grape harvest festival when people camped under little tents in the vineyards). Sometimes there was too much eating and drinking at feast time and the people had to be reminded of their religious meaning. *Amos 5. 21–24.*

Figs, as well as leaves, on the fig tree (p. 48)

FELIX. Roman governor of Judaea (A.D. 52–60) who tried Paul in Caesarea and kept him in prison for two years to please the Jews—probably hoping for a fat bribe to release him. *Acts 24. 22–26.*

FESTUS. The Roman official who succeeded Felix as governor of Judaea (A.D. 60–62) and eventually decided to send Paul for trial to Rome. *Acts 25. 12.*

FIG TREE. The fig tree is a favourite one in Bible lands. It gives shade as well as fruit. When Jesus was coming out of Bethany he saw a fig tree with a lot of leaves on it. This usually meant that somewhere amongst the leaves some ripe juicy figs were hidden, for leaves often come after the fruit on fig trees. But Jesus was disappointed, there were no figs, only a big show of leaves without fruit. *Mark 11. 12–14.*

FIRSTBORN. 'The firstborn of all creation.' This is Paul's way of describing the first place that is given to Jesus over everything. He chose the word 'firstborn' because all Jews understood how the eldest son was head of the family in place of the father. The firstborn had authority over his brothers and sisters. Those who believe in Jesus are also called 'firstborn' because they have entered the joys and responsibility of a new life. *Colossians 1. 15.*

FIRST FRUITS AND FIRSTLINGS. The Jewish people believed that all the produce of their farms and gardens came from God. In order to make this clear they brought early fruits and grain as well as the first lamb and the first calf of the year, to the Temple as gifts to God. After these first gifts had been consecrated they could then use the rest of the produce for themselves. *Exodus 23. 19.*

FISH AND FISHERMEN. Seven of Jesus' disciples were fishermen and were active in fishing in the Sea of Galilee. Much of their fishing was done with a big drag-net. Jesus

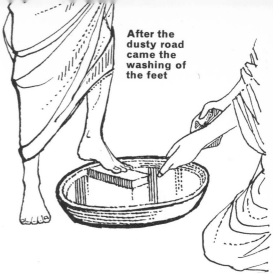

After the dusty road came the washing of the feet

promised that they would also become 'fishers of men', a phrase often used since to describe the work of Christ's disciples. *Matthew 4. 19.*

FLAX. When the spies of Joshua secretly entered Jericho they lived in the house of Rahab. In order to hide them from the king of the city she took them to the flat roof and hid them under long stalks of flax. She was drying out the flax before using it in linen weaving. Flax was also grown in Egypt, and is the oldest of all the fibres used in the textile industry. It grows lovely blue flowers. *Joshua 2. 1–14.*

FLOOD (see also *Ark*, *Dove* and *Noah*). 'For, behold, I will bring a flood of waters upon the earth.' This was God's decision to bring an end to the wickedness on the earth. According to the Bible story it rained for forty days and the flood lasted for one hundred and fifty days. Noah and his family, with two of every living creature, were housed in the Ark which rode on the waters and they were all saved. The Flood story is told to show God's anger at sin in the world and is a sign of his mercy towards men. God destroyed the world but also saved it and gave human beings a fresh start. *Genesis 6. 11–22.*

FOOTWASHING. 'He began to wash the disciples' feet.' In one of the last acts of his life Jesus performed the humblest task of all in any Jewish household. Palestine was a dusty land and people walked long distances in sandals and their feet got tired and dirty. When they arrived at a house a servant brought a basin for the foot washing. Jesus did it to show his disciples that the greatest among them should be the servant of all.
1 Samuel 25. 41; John 13. 3–11.

FORERUNNER. 'Jesus has gone on as a forerunner on our behalf.' This word is used only once in the New Testament. The forerunner was a scout, or messenger, sent on ahead of the army, or the chariot, to announce its coming. The word is often used by Christians to describe John the Baptist as the advance messenger of Christ. But it is Jesus himself who is the true forerunner preparing the way for us to follow. *Hebrews 6. 20.*

FORGIVENESS (see also *Debts*). 'Father, forgive them; for they know not what they do.' The cry of Jesus as he hung on the Cross was the cry of forgiveness. He was God's son and knew that his Father was a forgiving God. In the Old Testament Isaiah says God throws 'sins behind his back', and the prophet Micah speaks of God throwing 'sins into the deep sea'. Jesus said that men should 'forgive' one another when they had done wrong. He believed that forgiveness came first from God, for without his help, men could not forgive one another. Jesus put 'forgiveness' at the heart of the Lord's Prayer, for without that spirit we cannot be truly Christian.
Matthew 6. 12; Luke 23. 34.

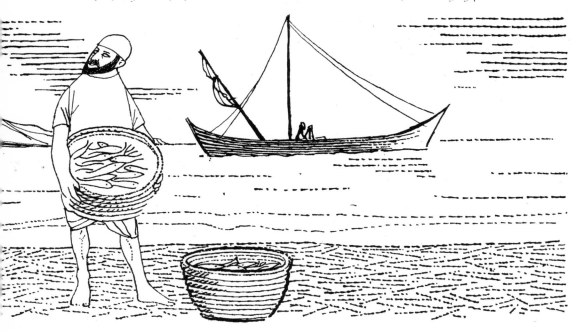

Fishermen who became fishers of men! Christ's first disciples were... (*next page*)

FRANKINCENSE (see also *Magicians*). At Bethlehem the wise men from the east presented frankincense to the new born Jesus. Frankincense is the whitish-yellow resin cut from the bark of the terebinth tree—a spreading tree that grows in warm, dry places in eastern countries. Frankincense has a pleasant smell and was used by the priests in the temple worship. *Matthew 2. 11.*

FRONTLETS. Sometimes called phylacteries. They were square pieces of hard calf's skin, or parchment, upon which passages of the Jewish law were written. Devout Jews then fastened the pieces to their foreheads so that everyone might see how much they respected the law. *Exodus 13. 16.*

FULLER. A fuller was the man who cleaned, or bleached, cloth as white as possible before it was dyed. He usually worked outside the walls of a city near a running stream, for he needed a lot of fresh water for his job. He washed the cloth in the stream using a kind of soap made of white clay. Then he spread the cloth to dry in the sun on the 'fuller's field'. *Mark 9. 3.*

FURLONG. A furlong is an eighth of a mile. When Jesus came walking on the sea to meet the disciples, they had rowed in their boat 25 or 30 furlongs, which is about 3 to 4 miles. *John 6. 19.*

FURNACE (see also *Abednego*). The furnace that the three young men—Shadrach, Meshach and Abednego—were thrown into, as described in the Book of Daniel, was probably used for baking bricks or smelting metal. Smaller furnaces, or crucibles, and ovens were used in homes. *Daniel 3. 13–27.*

G **GABBATHA.** When Pilate judged Jesus he did it at a spot called 'The Pavement', or, in the Hebrew language, 'Gabbatha', probably an open place outside the palace where the people could hear and see. *John 19. 13.*

GABRIEL. Only two angels are mentioned by name in the Bible—Gabriel and Michael. Gabriel is the messenger angel. He is sent to tell Mary about the birth of Jesus and to Zechariah to announce the birth of John the Baptist. Gabriel helps Daniel to understand his dreams, and Luke describes him as the angel that 'stands in the presence of God'. *Daniel 8. 16; Luke 1. 26–38.*

GAD. Gad was the seventh son of Jacob. His descendants, when they came into the Promised Land from Egypt, were allotted the hilly country to the east of the River Jordan. King David often found refuge amongst the wooded hills of Gad. *1 Samuel 13. 7.*

GADARENE (see also *Decapolis*). It was in the country district of the Gadarene people on the south-east side of the Sea of Galilee that Jesus performed one of his most notable miracles. He cast out the evil spirits of two 'devil possessed' men. The site of the Gadarene miracle was near the shore of the lake in the district of Gadara. *Mark 5. 1.*

GALATIANS, EPISTLE TO THE. Paul's letter to the Galatians is composed of six short chapters in the New Testament. He wrote it about A.D. 52 to the Christians who lived in the area called 'Galatia', now a part of Turkey. It has often been called the 'letter of liberty'. Paul pleads with his Galatian friends to break away from their old Jewish habits. He says that through their faith in Christ they are free men, and are no longer bound by old customs. Trying to keep the old law made them 'slaves', but Christ had made them free to follow his new law of love. *Epistle to the Galatians.*

GALILEE. The land of Christ's boyhood and of his early ministry. In Christ's day it was a province of the Roman Empire, about 40 miles from north to south, and 25 miles east to west. On the east its boundary was the Jordan Valley and the Sea of Galilee, and on the west the Mediterranean coast. It was a fertile, well-watered land, with

gentle limestone hills, growing grain and olives. Galilee is the background to many of Jesus' parables and stories. It was there he lived in his family and first preached the good news of the Gospel.
Matthew 13. 53–58; Luke 4. 14.

GALILEE, SEA OF. It was round the Sea of Galilee that Jesus loved to be, and on its shores he spent many memorable days. The lake is 13 miles long and 7 miles broad and is over 600 feet below sea-level. It is liable to sudden gusts of wind which whip the waters into violent storms. The River Jordan flows through it, and helps to keep its waters fresh and lively. Sometimes called the Lake of Gennesaret or the Sea of Tiberias and known as the 'sweet water' in contrast to the 'bitter water' of the Dead Sea. *Luke 5. 1–11.*

. . . skilled in the art of casting the great net which pulled in the big catches

GALL. When the Bible writers wished to refer to something bitter they called it 'gall'. There was a plant of that name with a bitter taste. Gall was mixed in the drink offered to Jesus on the Cross. *Matthew 27. 34.*

GAMALIEL. The early apostles in Jerusalem were brought before the priestly council of the Jews for preaching about Jesus. The majority of the council were so angry that they were ready to kill them. But one learned and respected member of the council—Gamaliel—warned its members to be careful what they did. If the new preaching was 'of men' it would fail. If it was 'of God' then no one could stop it. These wise words won the day and the apostles were released. *Acts 5. 33–39.*

GARDEN. Gardens are often mentioned in the Bible. The king's garden was a well-known landmark in Jerusalem with a wall round it, and a spring, or pool, for watering. Fruits, herbs, vegetables, olives and vines were cultivated in the gardens of the Bible. Sometimes in big gardens there was a summerhouse. A garden was often used as a burial place, and contained the family tomb. *2 Kings 25. 4; John 19. 41.*

GATH. 'Tell it not in Gath.' That phrase from David's lament over Saul and Jonathan is what is most remembered about Gath. It was one of the five main cities of the Philistines, and the home of the giant Goliath. David was anxious that the people of Gath should not rejoice over the death of Israel's leaders. *2 Samuel 1. 20.*

GAZA (see also *Dagon*). On the trade routes which run northwards from Egypt into Western Asia, Gaza was an important city. Joshua captured it from the Philistines when the Israelites came into Canaan but it often changed hands. It was in Gaza that the Philistines imprisoned Samson, and there he performed his last exploit in the destruction of the house in which the

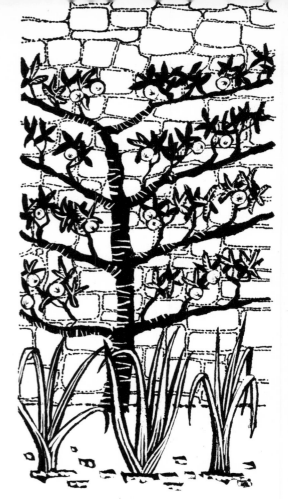

'With all choicest fruits - and water'

Philistines were feasting. *Judges 16. 21.*

GEDALIAH. When Nebuchadnezzar conquered the Israelites in 587 B.C., he appointed Gedaliah as governor of Judah. Gedaliah advised his countrymen to settle down and live peaceably under the new order. But some plotted against him and killed him. *2 Kings 25. 22–26.*

GEHAZI (see also *Naaman*). The servant of Elisha the prophet who on one occasion let greed get the better of him. When Naaman was cured of his leprosy by Elisha the prophet refused to take any gift. But Gehazi ran after Naaman and by telling a lie got a large present and hid it in his house. But Elisha knew what was

happening and as a punishment Gehazi himself was smitten with leprosy.
2 Kings 5. 18–27.

GENEALOGIES. In the Bible there are often long lists of names called 'genealogies' which give the history of the descent of an individual or a family. The Jews were very careful about these lists in order to show how exactly a man was descended. Both Matthew's and Luke's Gospels have their 'genealogy of Jesus Christ'. *1 Chronicles 9. 1; Matthew 1. 1; Luke 3. 23–38.*

GENESIS, BOOK OF. Genesis means 'beginning'. It introduces the story of man's redemption by God which runs all through the Bible. God is seen as the Creator of life and all things. He made man and gave man a world of wonder and beauty to live in. Man rebelled against God in sin and the world was drowned. But the casting forth of Adam and Eve from the Garden of Eden; the Great Flood; and the destruction of the Tower of Babel, did not remove man from God's mercy and care. With Abraham, Isaac and Jacob God moves to another stage in the redemption plan. He makes a 'covenant' with the People of Israel. God draws them to himself as his people. Through them the message of God's will for man continues to be proclaimed. Genesis is the great beginning of God's plan of salvation which leads on to its climax in Jesus Christ. It is a deeply 'religious' rather than a 'scientific' book. In it we see both God's loving purpose for man and man's response to God.
Book of Genesis.

GENTILES. The name, mentioned 117 times in the Bible, given to those people who are not Jews. It means 'nations' in general. But as the Jews became an exclusive and distinct people so 'Gentiles' referred only to non-Jews.
Acts 9. 15; Romans 15. 16.

'God made everything: it was very good'

'Are you still sleeping? Rise, let us be going; my betrayer is at hand'

GERIZIM. 'Our fathers worshipped on this mountain' said the Samaritan woman to Jesus, pointing to Mount Gerizim. Near the ancient city of Shechem the Samaritans still go up to the top to worship at the great festivals. *Deuteronomy 11. 29; John 4. 20.*

GETHSEMANE. 'And they went to a place called Gethsemane.' It was probably a spot on the Mount of Olives well known to Jesus and his disciples, away from the noise and bustle of Jerusalem and in a garden. There in the darkness of the early evening Jesus prayed to his Father while his tired disciples slept. It was there that Judas came to betray him. Mentioned only twice in the New Testament, Gethsemane is a name dear to the hearts of all Christians. *Matthew 26. 36; Mark 14. 32.*

GEZER. A town on the road between Joppa and Jerusalem given by the king of Egypt to his daughter who became Solomon's wife. *1 Kings 9. 16.*

GIANTS. 'And there we saw the giants; the sons of Anak.' So ran the report of the spies sent into Palestine by Moses. These large sons of Anak, the most famous giants of the Bible, frightened the spies so much that they said, 'We seemed to look like grasshoppers.' These men of big stature impressed the Jewish invaders who were probably people of medium build. *Numbers 13. 30–33.*

GIBEON. The ancestral home of King Saul about six miles north of Jerusalem. Said to be the modern el-Jib, the site has yielded many archaeological discoveries. When the conquering Israelites came to Gibeon, the people of Gibeon were very frightened. Could they escape the fate of Jericho and Ai? They planned a clever trick. They put on their old clothes, loaded their donkeys with worn-out sacks, cracked wine-skins, and mouldy bread. 'Look,' they said to Joshua, 'we've come a long journey to make a treaty of friendship with you.'

Joshua believed them and made the treaty. But when he came to Gibeon he discovered the same men and was angry at their deception. He condemned them to be forever slaves to the people of Israel—'hewers of wood and drawers of water.' *Joshua 9. 3–27.*

GIDEON. A farmer-soldier-hero of the Old Testament. As Gideon threshed his wheat secretly in the wine-press for fear of the Midianites the angel of God commanded him to defy the oppression of the Midianites. With ten of his servants he pulled down the altar of Midian's god. Then rallying the tribe he collected an army of 10,000. 'Too many men,' said God. So Gideon asked his men to drink at a stream,

and noticed that some lapped up the water with their hands while others knelt down and put their mouths right into the stream. He chose the 300 alert men who lapped and with them defeated the enemy. The Israelites wanted him to become king but Gideon refused. *Judges 6–8.*

Those who lapped were the lively ones

GILBOA. Amongst the mountains of Gilboa in the north of Palestine Saul fought his final battle with the Philistines and was killed. David mentions Gilboa in his beautiful lament for Saul and Jonathan. *1 Samuel 31. 1–8.*

GILEAD (see also *Balm*). This is the general name given to the lands on the east side of the River Jordan occupied by the tribes of Reuben, Gad and Manasseh. Its wooded hills provided hiding places for fugitives. Jacob fled to Gilead and so did David. *Genesis 31. 21–55; 2 Samuel 17. 22ff.*

GILGAL. When they crossed the River Jordan into the Promised Land the Israelites

55

**Leave a little
of the harvest
for others**

made Gilgal their headquarters. Twelve
stones—one for each tribe—were set up in
Gilgal and from there Joshua planned his
attack on Jericho which is close at hand.
At Gilgal the tribes were allotted their
lands and there they celebrated the first
Passover in their new home. They looked
back on the camp at Gilgal as a historic
place in their history. *Joshua 4.*

GIRDLE (see also *Ephod*). A ceremonial
sash, or belt, made of embroidered linen
and in many colours, worn by the high
priest and other dignitaries in the Temple.
Leathern girdles were worn by workers to
tuck up their clothes, and by warriors as a
belt for sheath and sword.
Exodus 28. 4; Mark 1. 6.

GIRGASHITES. One of the tribes of
Canaan which were eventually overcome
by the invading Israelites. *Joshua 3. 10.*

GLEANING. A kindly law of Israel allowed poor people to go into the fields at
harvest time to collect, or glean, ears of
barley and ripe olives and grapes which the
harvesters missed.
Deuteronomy 24. 19–22; Ruth 2. 2ff.

GOAD. A long handled, pointed instrument used to urge on the oxen when
ploughing. The Israelite warrior Shamgar
used a goad to kill six hundred Philistines.
Judges 3. 31.

GOAT. The goat is a popular animal in
the Bible and is mentioned over a hundred
times. The goat provided milk, hair for
weaving cloth and skins for leather. Little
goats (kids) were tender as meat. No wonder there was a herd of goats on every farm,
for goats could find food in the most wild
and desolate places. The goat was often
used as a sacrificial animal. *Proverbs 30. 31.*

GOD. The Bible is the book of God. It is
all about him and the ways in which he

**Man's four footed
friends. They
give him food,
drink, clothing
and transport**

makes himself known to men. The Hebrews used the name *Yahweh* for God, which our English Bibles sometimes translate as *Jehovah*. The Bible writers assume the presence of God, his Being and his Character. He is a Spirit. He is a Holy God. He is the Creator of life. He is Judge of the Earth. He loves the good and hates the evil. He expects his worshippers to be like that too. God makes himself finally clear in the New Testament in Jesus Christ. Jesus reveals him as Father. He shows God's mercy, forgiveness and love. The character of God is summed up in one word—Love. *The Bible.*

GOLGOTHA (see *Calvary*). An Aramaic word meaning 'skull' and a name for the hill where Jesus was crucified. It may be because skulls were found there, or that it was a place of execution. The probable site is inside the present wall of Jerusalem. *Matthew 27. 33.*

GOLIATH. A giant serving in the Philistine army whose home was in the town of Gath. He was said to stand ten feet high and was dressed in a colossal suit of armour. He carried a spear as big as the wooden beam a weaver used, with its head weighing twenty pounds. But Goliath's forehead was unprotected. David the shepherd boy aimed the stone in his sling at that spot and stunned the giant. He ran quickly forward and with the giant's own sword killed Goliath. *1 Samuel 17. 4–54.*

GOMER. A grandson of Noah and the eldest son of Japheth. Hosea's wife was called Gomer. *Genesis 10. 2; Hosea 1. 3.*

GOMORRAH (see also *Lot, Sodom*). 'Then the Lord rained on Sodom and Gomorrah brimstone and fire from the Lord out of heaven; and he overthrew those cities.' Gomorrah was one of the evil cities of the plain of Jordan, probably situated at the southern tip of the Dead Sea. About two thousand years before Jesus a tremendous earthquake changed the face of the plain and ruined the cities. It may be that their ruins lie beneath the waters of the Dead Sea. The Bible writers record this event as a punishment by God for the wickedness of the cities. *Genesis 19. 24–29.*

GOPHER WOOD. Noah's Ark was made of gopher wood which is probably the same as cypress. *Genesis 6. 14.*

'David prevailed with a sling and a stone'

GOSHEN. The area in Egypt where the Israelites lived was called Goshen and was in the eastern part of the Nile delta. An area in southern Palestine was also called Goshen. *Genesis 47. 6.*

GOSPEL, GOSPELS. Gospel means 'good news', and the 'good news' of the Gospels is that Jesus Christ is the Son of God. The word occurs seventy-five times in the New Testament. The Four Gospels (Matthew, Mark, Luke and John) are four records of this 'gospel'. They record what the Christian church remembered about the 'gospel' (Jesus Christ). The 'Gospels' speak about the coming of Jesus, what he did, how he lived, how he died and rose from the dead; they testify to the truth of the 'gospel'. The earliest of the Gospel writers is Mark. Matthew and Luke use some of what he wrote. John put down his remembrances very much later—it is more a book of reflection and meditation. Taken together the four Gospels give us a true word record of the 'good news' that is Jesus Christ.
Gospels of Matthew, Mark, Luke and John.

GOURD. Jonah sat under a gourd tree out of the sun. God made it grow to give him some shade. It may have been a little tree like a 'castor-oil' plant or a larger tree like a vine. *Jonah 4. 6.*

GRACE. One of the great words of the Bible which occurs again and again in the Old and New Testaments, and has many different shades of meaning. It can mean 'mercy', 'loving kindness', 'forgiveness'. It describes God's attitude to man. It can also be used to describe the relationship between one man and another. The Bible records a 'gracious' religion for it describes God's love towards us even when we do not deserve it. *Romans 3. 21–26.*

GRAPES. Palestine has always been a land of the vine. Its vineyards produce an abundance of grapes as the Israelite spies discovered when they brought back bunches of luscious grapes to Moses and Aaron. *Numbers 13. 23.*

GRAVEN IMAGE (see also *Idols*). 'Thou shalt not make unto thee any graven image.' This commandment, amongst the Ten Commandments, was faithfully obeyed by the Jews. They were not to set up 'images' or 'gods' to be seen and worshipped. That was idolatry. Their God was the living God, unseen but always present. That belief has been continued into Christian worship. *Exodus 20. 4.*

Greece—the land of Heroes, Philosophers, Artists and Sculptors. In design, style and thought Greece led the world

The olive crowned the Greek
athlete and gave oil for
every home (see also OLIVE)

GREECE, GREEKS. Greece and the Greeks are mentioned over thirty times in the Bible. When Jesus was crucified the accusation against him was written in Greek letters on the Cross as well as in Hebrew and Latin. Greek civilization and philosophy spread through the lands of the Bible. Christianity was greatly influenced by them. Some of the earliest Christian churches were started in Greece. Today the Greek Orthodox Church is one of the great churches of the Christian world. *Acts 17. 4; 20. 2.*

GUEST-CHAMBER (see also *Elisha*). Hospitality to friends and kindness to strangers are taken for granted all the way through the Bible. In many homes there was a 'guest-chamber' for the visitor. There, after the kiss of welcome and washing of the feet, he could rest in quietness. On the night of his arrest Jesus guided his disciples to a guest-room he was familiar with in Jerusalem, where supper had been prepared. *Mark 14. 14.*

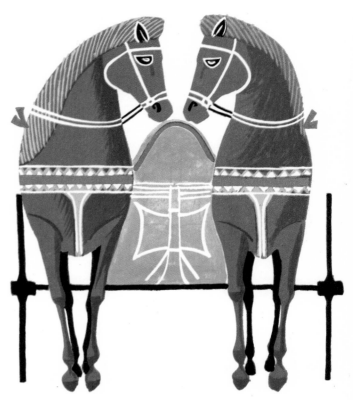

HABAKKUK. The Book of Habakkuk, near the end of the Old Testament, consists of three short chapters in the form of a poem or psalm. Little is known of the man who wrote it. He stands on his watch tower and sees the Babylonians as masters of the world and wonders why God allows them to carry out their cruel and barbarous plans on the Hebrew people. It all seems to be a denial of God's goodness. At last the prophet sees that their pride will be the downfall of the enemy and that God's faithful people will be saved. Habakkuk probably wrote about six hundred years before Christ. *Book of Habakkuk.*

HAGGAI. The Book of Haggai consists of two short chapters almost at the end of the Old Testament. They were probably written by Haggai after he returned from exile, about 520 years before Christ. He was depressed at the appearance of the Temple and challenged the Jews to re-build it before they built their own houses. His prophecy is a reminder to the people of the greatness of God and that God deserves the best they can give. *Book of Haggai.*

HAIL. A great storm of hail stones was one of the 'plagues' which descended on Egypt in the days of the Israelite captivity. When Moses raised his rod the hail fell from the sky and ruined the crops of the Egyptians. But the Israelites, in the land of Goshen, were saved from the destruction as a sign of God's favour towards them.
Exodus 9. 22–26.

HALLELUJAH. A Hebrew word used in worship meaning 'praise ye God', or 'praise the Lord'. It occurs 24 times in the Psalms, and the Book of Revelation. It is a word often used in Christian worship.
Revelation 19. 1–6.

HAM. One of the sons of Noah whose descendants lived in North Africa and Arabia and from whom people there are said to be descended. *Genesis 5. 32.*

HAMAN (see also *Esther*). In the Book of Esther Haman is the proud servant of the king of Persia who becomes furiously angry because Mordecai the Jew does not bow down before him. He plans to hang Mordecai and massacre the Jews. But Esther tells the king of the plan. Instead of Mordecai, Haman himself is hanged and the Jews are saved. *Esther 7. 1–10.*

HAMATH. A town which guarded the northern entry to Israel—the modern Hama of Syria. *Numbers 13. 21.*

HAND. The Bible refers to the 'hand' many hundreds of times, and in scores of different ways. The 'hand' suggested power and might. People settled an agreement by shaking hands, and the lifting of the hand meant action. The touch of a hand was used in blessing or healing and then both hands were often used. The 'hand' of God, or the Lord, suggested the power of God. Jesus used his hands to perform miracles and so did his disciples. The use of the hands in the Bible showed there was a close re-lation between what today we call 'body' and 'spirit'.

Joshua 8. 19; 1 Kings 11. 26; Mark 6. 5; Acts 8. 17–19.

HANNAH (see also *Eli, Samuel*). The mother of Samuel, the boy who became the prophet-judge of Israel. She vowed that if she had a son she would dedicate him to the service of God in the Temple. Her song of thanksgiving is one of the loveliest poems in the Old Testament, and has its counterpart in the song of Mary (the Magnificat) in Luke's Gospel.

1 Samuel 2. 1–10.

HARAN. 'My brothers, where do you come from?' 'We are from Haran.' That simple question and answer led to a great discovery for Jacob. In his wanderings he had reached the important town of Haran. It had ample grass and water. The herdsmen he met told him of Laban his uncle and his beautiful daughter Rachel. In the country of Haran, the upper part of the Euphrates river valley,

'Hail, very heavy hail such as had never been in Egypt, struck down every plant of the field'

Jacob worked for Laban for fourteen years and eventually married Rachel. Haran, on the trade route to the sea, was also well known to Abraham and Lot. Modern excavations have helped to reveal its ancient past. *Genesis 29. 4–30.*

HARP. 'David took the harp and played it with his hand.' That is perhaps the most famous instance in the Bible where the harp (or lyre) is used. David played to soothe the distracted spirit of King Saul. The harp is the first musical instrument mentioned in the Bible (Genesis 4. 21). The number of its strings is not certain. They could be plucked by the hand, or with an instrument called the plectrum. *1 Samuel 16. 23.*

HARROW. A farming implement made of wood with strong pointed teeth. It was dragged along the ground by oxen in order to break up the clods of earth after ploughing. *Isaiah 28. 24.*

HARVEST. The Bible lands were farming lands and harvest was one of the great seasons. In the hot valley of the Jordan the crops of barley were harvested in April and May and the wheat later. All the harvesting was done by hand with the sickle. The ripe handfuls were tied in bundles and then into the bigger sheaves. Then they were loaded on to donkeys and carried to the threshing floor. The sheaves were laid out on the floor and the donkeys trampled on them to loosen the ripe grain. Then the farmer and his helpers tossed the heaps into the wind with wooden pitchforks. The wind blew away the light chaff leaving only the good grain and the straw on the threshing floor. The grain was put into bags to make bread and cakes and the straw was used for animal feeding. Crops of cucumbers, melons, beans, lentils, olives, figs and nuts were also part of the harvest. *Isaiah 17. 5–6.*

HATE, HATRED. These words occur many times in the Bible and with different meanings. In the Old Testament 'hatred' usually means 'dislike'. In the New Testament 'hate' is often contrasted with 'love'

**Harvest - from the
reaper in the field to
the good grain
on the threshing floor**

to show the positive power of love.
Psalm 97. 10; Luke 6. 22; John 15. 18ff.

HAZAEL. A powerful king of Syria who often invaded the land of Israel in the days of King Jehu and the prophet Elisha. The prophet saw him as a sign of God's anger against Israel for her wrong-doing.
2 Kings 13. 3.

HAZEL. Another name for the lovely almond tree whose pink blossoms come as early as January in the Holy Land.
Genesis 30. 37.

HAZOR. Hazor, a town in Galilee, was the scene of one of Joshua's most famous victories. He defeated King Jabin of Hazor, who came out against the Israelites with many horses and chariots, and burnt the city. Solomon restored and fortified Hazor but later the Assyrians captured and destroyed it. All these happenings make Hazor of fascinating interest to the archaeologists who have dug deep into its past.
Joshua 11. 1–15.

HEART. For the Bible writers the 'heart' is the centre of life. It represented everything that a man is—his character, his will, his mind—all that made him a person. The 'heart' governed all his actions. The 'heart' was not thought of as a separate physical organ. It always referred to life itself. The word occurs nearly a thousand times in the Bible.
Deuteronomy 11. 13; Matthew 5. 8; Acts 4. 32.

HEATHEN (see also *Gentiles*). The Bible writers distinguished between the Hebrew people and the rest of mankind who were sometimes called 'heathen' or 'Gentiles'. In some translations of the Bible the word means 'nations'.
Psalm 47. 8; Galatians 1. 16.

HEAVEN. 'I have sinned against heaven.' That cry was from the Prodigal Son as he came home to his father's house. His sin was against God but the word 'heaven' shows how the Bible writers thought of 'heaven'. It was the place where God is. To the Gospel writers 'kingdom of God' and 'kingdom of heaven' are the same.

'Praise him sun and moon, and all you shining stars'

'Heaven' is also sky, sun, moon, stars and the expanse of space above the earth. One day, God had promised, all of this would disappear and there would be a 'new heaven and a new earth'.
Deuteronomy 26. 15; Revelation 21.

HEBREW. Hebrew is the ancient language of the Jews; and most of the Old Testament was written in it. Hebrew is written and read from right to left. Many words used in English came originally from Hebrew, such as: sabbath, sack, satan, jubilee.
Luke 23. 33; Acts 21. 40.

HEBREWS. The Bible uses this word to describe Abraham and his descendants. It was their name as captives in Egypt, and as they gradually grew into a nation through the period of the Exodus the name stuck to them. By the time of Christ the name was used to describe all Jews whether they lived in Palestine or outside it. It distinguished them from the Romans and the Greeks.
Genesis 14. 13; Philippians 3. 5.

HEBREWS, EPISTLE TO. 'Let us run with perseverance the race that is set before us, looking to Jesus the pioneer and perfecter of our faith.' That sentence from the Epistle to the Hebrews is the key to this wonderful piece of writing in the New Testament. The unknown writer is reminding his friends that Jesus Christ is superior to everything and everyone. His friends may have been Jewish Christians who had been tempted to slip back again into their Jewish ways and customs. But whoever they were the 'Writer to the Hebrews' wrote them a powerful 'letter' which all the centuries of Christianity have valued. It is one of the greatest of the New Testament writings and was probably written about sixty years after the Resurrection of Christ.
Epistle to the Hebrews.

HEBRON. Nineteen miles south-west of Jerusalem, and standing on a hill over three thousand feet above sea-level, Hebron was an ancient place even in Abraham's day. Abraham was buried there, and the Patriarch's sepulchre site is pointed out to visitors today. It was one of the strongholds of the Sons of Anak, the giants who so frightened the Israelitish spies. In Hebron David became king, and Hebron was his capital for over seven years. There his son Absalom stirred up rebellion against his father. Hebron was a memorable and historic place for the Jewish people.
Genesis 23. 19–20; 2 Samuel 5. 1–5.

HEIR. 'This is the heir; come let us kill him.' In that sentence Mark records one of the most dramatic parables Jesus told. It was about the man who sent his servants to inspect his vineyard. Some were beaten and some were killed by the tenants. Then at last he sent his son and they killed him in the belief that they would inherit the vineyard. The heir was usually the eldest son and the story points to Jesus himself. He is the heir to all things and with him we share the divine inheritance both in this life and the next. *Mark 12. 7–8; Romans 8. 17.*

HELL (see also *Hinnom*). This word is used in the Bible to cover three different meanings—*Sheol*, *Hades* and *Gehenna*. The first simply means 'the place of the dead' and is the most common. The second refers to the world of the dead, the underworld, a region underneath the earth; while the third refers to a place of everlasting punishment for sinners.
Genesis 37. 35; Matthew 5. 22; Acts 2. 27.

HEM OF GARMENT. A Jewish robe had a wide 'hem' or 'fringe'. Some hems were beautifully embroidered and had a border of tassels bound by a coloured cord. Anyone who wished to show how religious he was put a very wide hem on his garments.
Deuteronomy 22. 12; Matthew 9. 20.

HEPHZIBAH. In his beautiful poem about the future glory of Israel Isaiah gives the nation a number of striking names. One of them is Hephzibah—meaning 'My delight is in her'—a favourite name amongst Hebrew women. *Isaiah 62. 3–5.*

HERD. Men in the Old Testament often counted their wealth in herds of cattle. Herdsmen guarded the herds and drove them to the places where there was plenty of grass and water. *Genesis 18. 7.*

HERMON. Far to the north of the Sea of Galilee, and at the meeting place of modern Israel, Lebanon and Syria, Mount Hermon rises to over 9000 feet. Its snow gives water to the Jordan. It may be the 'Mount of Transfiguration' (but see Tabor). *Psalm 133. 3.*

'If only I touch his garment I shall be made well'—the woman's faith was triumphant

King only in name, under the Romans, Herod loved to show off his royal dignity in chariots and great buildings

HEROD. Under the Roman Empire Herod the Great was given the title 'King of the Jews', much to the annoyance of the Jews who disliked him because he came from Idumea or Edom and not from Israel. It was during his reign that Jesus was born in Bethlehem. Herod died soon afterwards, and his son Herod Antipas ruled in the Galilee part of the land. He imprisoned and executed John the Baptist and Jesus was brought to him for a brief trial. Another of the Herods, a grandson of Herod the Great, later attacked the apostles in Jerusalem in order to please the Jews and fell down dead as he made a speech from his throne. *Matthew 2; Luke 23. 6–12; Acts 12.*

HERODIANS. 'Is it lawful to pay taxes to Caesar?' The crafty Herodians, a political group supporting the Herod royal family, hoped to trick Jesus by their question. If he said 'Yes' they would hate and oppose him for not being a good nationalist Jew. If he said 'No' they could report him to the Roman governor. Jesus answered, 'Render unto Caesar the things that are Caesar's, and to God the things that are God's.' *Matthew 22. 16.*

HERODIAS (see also *Herod*). King Herod (Antipas) had married Herodias the wife of his half-brother, which John the Baptist said was not lawful. This angered Herodias who laid a clever plot against the prophet. Her daughter (she may have been Salome) danced before Herod and so pleased him that he promised to give the girl whatever she asked for. Egged on by her mother she asked for the head of John the Baptist on a platter, and the beheading was immediately carried out. *Mark 6. 14–29.*

HEZEKIAH. 'And he did that which was right in the eyes of the Lord.' This is the Bible's tribute to Hezekiah, one of the best kings that Judah ever had. He was a young man of 25 when his reign began and 54 when he died, in 687 B.C. He re-opened the Temple and made it fit for worship and under him all the Jewish festivals were kept with much ceremony. He did away with the big bronze serpent which had become an idol of worship as a reminder of their wilderness wanderings. He built up the defences of Jerusalem and brought water into the city. The Jews looked back to Hezekiah's days with much gratitude. *2 Kings 18–20.*

HIGH PLACE. What was a 'high place' in the Bible? There are many meanings. Sometimes it means a 'mountain-top', a

'shrine' or a place of 'sacrifice'. But it also came to mean a place of idol-worship specially built to a local god. Upright stones and pillars were placed on high ground and attracted people to worship them as 'local gods'. *2 Kings 21. 3.*

HIGH PRIEST (see also *Caiaphas*). The office of high priest was by Jewish tradition vested in the family of Eleazar, the son of

Aaron. But by the time of Jesus it had become an appointment made by the ruling Roman power.
Numbers 4. 16; Mark 14. 53.

HILKIAH. He was high priest during the reign of the young king Josiah (640–609 B.C.). During the repairs to the Temple in 622 B.C. he found the scrolls of the Law Book (Deuteronomy) hidden within the building and brought it to the king. They read it together and were inspired to bring about many reforms in the life and worship of the people. *2 Kings 22.*

and Solomon. He sent his expert carpenters and masons to help in the building of the Temple as well as supplies of cedar wood from the forests of Lebanon. Solomon's ships and Hiram's ships went off on expeditions in search of gold and silver, ivory, apes and peacocks.
2 Samuel 5. 11; 1 Kings 10. 22.

HIRELING. 'He flees because he is a hireling and cares nothing for the sheep.' In the parable of the Good Shepherd, as told in John's Gospel, the shepherd is prepared to lay down his life for the sheep against the

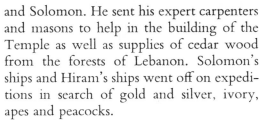

Wonderful cargoes came home in the ships of Hiram and Solomon

HINNOM, VALLEY OF. The Valley lies to the south of Jerusalem and was used for idol worship. It was sometimes also used for burning corpses of criminals and animals and for the disposal of refuse. It had a gloomy and frightening reputation and was often thought of as the 'mouth of hell'.
Joshua 15. 8; Jeremiah 32. 35.

HIRAM. King of Tyre and friend of David

attack of the wolf. But the hired shepherd was often not trustworthy and thought only of his own safety.
Job 7. 1–2; John 10. 11–15.

HITTITES. When Abraham came to Hebron he made a bargain with the Hittites, who lived in the region, for a piece of land as a burial ground. He paid 400 shekels of silver worth about 260 dollars

67

Even the smell is honey!

or 85 pounds. The Hittites were descended from a once mighty Hittite empire in Asia Minor. They mixed well with the Israelites when the Israelites came into the Promised Land. One of David's mighty warriors was Uriah, the Hittite. *Genesis 23. 3–16.*

HIVITES. People who lived in the hills of Lebanon beyond Israel and who often came to work across the border. Some of them worked for King Solomon. *1 Kings 9. 20.*

HOLINESS. Holiness in the Bible always has to do with God. It is the word that describes his 'separateness' from man; his purity; his difference from all other gods and all other created things. There are also places called 'holy'. They are given that name because they have to do with God who is holy. Jesus Christ is the supreme instance of what we mean by 'holy' in life and character. *Psalm 29. 2; Luke 1. 75.*

HOLY SPIRIT (see also *Spirit*). Spirit is one of the greatest words in the Bible meaning the very 'life-breath' of something living. So Holy Spirit is the 'life-breath' of the God who is Holy. The Old Testament thinks of the 'spirit' giving power. In the New Testament 'Holy Spirit' comes to the disciples of Christ at Pentecost and gives them power. It is the new power of Christ in his church. Christians think of God as Holy Spirit. With the Father, and the Son, Holy Spirit makes up the fullness of God. *Psalm 139. 7–12; Acts 2. 1–4.*

HONEY. A favourite food in Bible times —found in the hollows of rocks and trees, and often thought of as the sweetest of sweet things. *Psalm 19. 10; Matthew 3. 4.*

HOPE. In the Bible hope is always linked to faith in God, for without that it has no real foundation. Jesus himself says little about 'hope' in his teaching. But because of Jesus and his Resurrection we have the greatest hope of all—in a life beyond death and assurance of his coming again. Paul

68

refers to 'faith, hope and love' as the three abiding Christian qualities. *1 Corinthians 13. 13; 1 Peter 1. 3.*

HORNS. The ram, the goat, the wild-ox, all had horns and were respected by the Bible writers for their strength. So the word 'horn' came to be thought of as a symbol for power and strength. The Bible speaks of the 'horn' of the righteous man, the 'horn' of the wicked, the 'horn' of David, the 'horn' of salvation, the 'horns of the nations'. *Zechariah 1. 18–21; Luke 1. 69.*

HOSANNA. A shout of welcome and greeting used at the triumphal entry of Jesus into Jerusalem. It means 'save, we beseech thee'. *Psalm 118. 25; Matthew 21. 9.*

HOSEA. The prophecy of Hosea in the Old Testament tells the story of a man whose own 'love story' went wrong. We know little of Hosea himself apart from his poem-prophecy of fourteen short chapters which he wrote about 700 years before Christ. His own love for his erring wife Gomer shines through the writings to show how a good man continued to love through all trouble. It is a tender, affectionate book. Hosea also sees God continuing to love the People of Israel in spite of their waywardness. Hosea hopes that Israel will return to the ways of God. He hopes too for the love once again of his wife. *Book of Hosea.*

HOUSE. In Bible times houses were usually just two storeys in height with a flat roof. Walls were thick and the building materials were sun-dried bricks. Furniture varied according to the wealth of the owner. The basic equipment was a table, a chair and a reed mat for sleeping. The rich would have a couch or bed. The oven for cooking was sometimes outside in the courtyard, and much of the life of the house was lived outside in the warm weather. By the time of Jesus houses had got bigger and better furnished even in the smaller villages, and amongst poorer people in country places. *Matthew 7. 24–27.*

Hyssop   **Cummin**   **Anise**   **Coriander**

**Flowering and
fragrant plants
grew in the courtyards
of Hebrew houses**

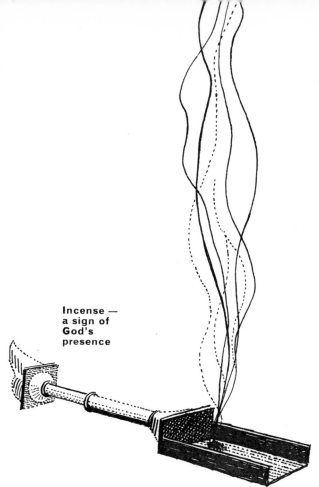

Incense —
a sign of
God's
presence

HUSBANDMAN. This word is used in the Bible to describe the man who 'farms' or 'tills'. He may be the owner-farmer himself or the man he employs. God himself is spoken of as the 'husbandman' of the true vine and of the church.
John 15. 1; 1 Corinthians 3. 9.

HYPOCRITE. One who professes to be good when he knows that he is not. Jesus was very angry with people of this kind. On one occasion he told his listeners to watch out for the log in their own eyes before bothering about the speck of dirt in someone else's. He always warned his friends about making a great display of their religion in case they fell into hypocrisy.
Matthew 6. 2; Luke 6. 41–42.

HYSSOP. A bushy herb with a sharp, spicy scent. The Biblical hyssop has not

been fully identified with any modern plant. *Psalm 51. 7.*

ICHABOD. This Hebrew word occurs only once in the Bible. It means 'where is the glory?' It was the name given by his mother to the little grandson of Eli, the old priest. The baby was born on the day that the Philistines captured the Ark of God from the Israelites. It was a very sad day for Eli's family, for they were responsible for the Ark which was the most precious possession the Israelites had. On sad occasions today people sometimes say, 'Ichabod. The glory has departed.'
1 Samuel 4. 19-22.

ICONIUM. A city in Asia Minor visited by Paul and Barnabas on their missionary tours. The people were keenly interested in what the two men said. Some were for, and some against the apostles. Eventually they had to leave the city for fear of causing a riot. *Acts 14. 1–7.*

IDOLS (see also *Graven Image*). An idol is an image in wood, stone or metal which represents a 'god'. In the Bible we read of the people of Israel worshipping mountains, springs, trees and blocks of stone, and a golden calf. But they were warned against doing this. It could lead to idol worship. The one true God of Israel did not need an 'image' in stone or wood, or metal. That was a 'false god'. The second commandment condemned idol worship.
Exodus 20. 4–5; Isaiah 40. 18ff.

IDUMEA (see also *Edom*). The southern part of the land of Judah where some of the descendants of Esau, called Edomites, lived. *Isaiah 34. 5ff.*

IMMANUEL. 'They shall call his name Immanuel, which means God is with us.' This was the prophecy fulfilled through Mary and announced just before Jesus was born. The Bible mentions this wonderful name for Jesus only three times—twice in Isaiah's prophecy and once in Matthew. The

name means exactly what it says, for, in Jesus, 'God is with us'.

Isaiah 7. 14; Matthew 1. 23.

INCENSE. In their worship of God the people of Israel were commanded to make a 'sweet smoke' in the Temple. It was a sign of God's presence and made the Temple smell of a nice perfume.

Leviticus 16. 12–13.

INHERITANCE. The words *inherit* and *inheritance* are often mentioned in the Bible. They refer to what 'belongs' to a person or to a nation. They mean the possessions which people have. When the people of Israel came into the Promised Land it is described as their 'inheritance'. In the New Testament Christians are described as those who 'inherit' the kingdom of God. Jesus himself is also described as the one who 'inherits' all things from God.

Deuteronomy 12. 10; Matthew 25. 34.

INN. The inn was usually a simple place of shelter in Bible times. The first mention of it comes in the story of Joseph in the Book of Genesis. Joseph's brothers on their way home from Egypt stopped to feed their donkeys at an inn and discovered money in their sacks. The inn at Bethlehem had no room for Mary and Joseph. To the inn on the Jerusalem–Jericho road the Good Samaritan brought the man who had been 'beaten up' by robbers.

Genesis 42. 27; Luke 2. 7; 10. 34.

ISAAC (see also *Abraham*). When Abraham was told that he was to have a son he laughed, and so did Sarah his wife, for they

Abraham took the ram and sacrificed it instead of Isaac

'I saw the Lord high and lifted up'—Isaiah

of 'Abraham, Isaac and Jacob', and the God and Father of Jesus Christ whom we worship today.
Genesis 17. 17; 21. 1–3.

ISAIAH, BOOK OF. Amongst the Old Testament prophets Isaiah is one of the foremost. He lived and worked in Jerusalem about 700 years before Christ and may have been born into the royal family. His writings are divided into different sections. Much of it is in the form of poems. Isaiah preaches that God is 'holy', and that he expects his people of Israel to be like that too. God is angry with the people because of their sin but he does not turn his back on them completely. There are always 'the few' worth saving. Isaiah also looks forward to a golden age for Israel when the long expected king, or Messiah, will come to bring in peace and happiness in all the world.
Book of Isaiah.

ISHBOSHETH. A son of King Saul whose name means 'man of shame' was for a time king of Israel after his father's death in 1000 B.C. David was his enemy. Two of Ishbosheth's officers killed him as he lay resting on his bed. They brought his head to David thinking that David would be very pleased. But he was angry at the cowardly way in which they had done the deed, and ordered them to be killed too.
2 Samuel 4. 5–12.

ISHMAEL. A son of Abraham. His mother Hagar was a serving maid of Abraham's wife, Sarah. According to the custom of the

were too old to have children. When the boy was born they called him 'Isaac' which means 'one laughs'. Abraham was very proud of his little son. God promised that through Isaac a great nation should arise. Abraham's faith was tested when God commanded him to offer Isaac as a sacrifice but at the final moment a ram appeared to be sacrificed in place of Isaac. From Isaac's marriage with Rebecca came Esau and Jacob and from Jacob, later called Israel, the Israelite people are descended. Through Isaac God was at work establishing his 'covenant' with his people. God is the God

Israel learned to be united as one people . . .

time, since Sarah did not have a son, Ishmael was the heir. But when Isaac was born to Sarah the two mothers became jealous. At last Abraham was compelled to send Ishmael and his mother away. They nearly died of thirst in the desert but God heard the cry of the little boy Ishmael, and his mother was guided to a well of water. Ishmael grew up to be an archer, married an Egyptian woman and had many sons. *Genesis 16. 15; 25. 12–16.*

ISRAEL. The new name given to Jacob following the night of his meeting with God. 'Thy name shall be called no more Jacob but Israel.' It means 'God strives'. Jacob's twelve sons became the 'fathers' of the twelve tribes which composed the 'people', or 'nation', or 'children of Israel'.

After their slavery in Egypt God led them into the Promised Land. In these long years of wandering across the wilderness they gradually became 'one people' linked to 'one God'. They had to fight for their lives against their enemies in the Promised Land, but under King David and King Solomon they were united as a strong nation. Then came the invasions of Israel from Assyria and Babylon. Many Israelites were carried off into captivity. About sixty years before Jesus was born the Romans conquered Israel. All during these years Israel never forgot that they were more than a nation; they were a 'people of God' specially chosen by him. They believed he would send to them his 'Messiah'—his 'anointed one'. But when he came—in the person of Jesus—Israel failed to recognize him. *Genesis 32. 22–32; Luke 1. 68–79.*

ISSACHAR. A son of Jacob (Israel) and Leah, and the ancestor of one of the twelve tribes of Israel. Their land lay in the rich plain of Jezreel. *Genesis 49. 14–15.*

ISSUE OF BLOOD (see also *Hem of Garment*). As Jesus was walking through the streets of Capernaum a woman touched the hem of his garment. She had suffered for many years from a haemorrhage which meant a loss of much blood. But her faith made her come near to Jesus. She believed that if only she could touch him she would be healed. Although there were a lot of people round him Jesus noticed what the woman did. He said to her, 'Be of good cheer, your faith has made you well again.' *Matthew 9. 20–22.*

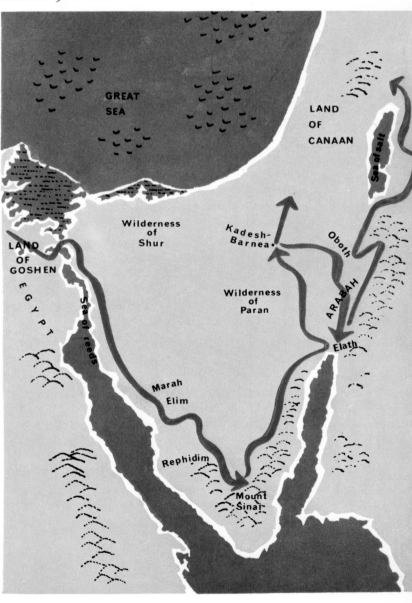

. . . as they marched through the desert from Egypt to Canaan

73

ITTAI. A soldier who refused to leave King David at the time when many of his men were deserting. David's son Absalom was in rebellion against his father and many soldiers were going over to his side. 'Why don't you go too?' said David. Then Ittai replied with a noble answer, 'In what place my lord the king shall be, whether in death or life, even there also will thy servant be.' Although he was not an Israelite Ittai became one of David's generals.
2 Samuel 15. 19–21.

IVORY. The ivory mentioned in the Old Testament came over the Syrian desert trade routes from the lands of the upper Euphrates River. The ivory tusks of elephants were very valuable. To have ivory in your house was a sign of wealth. Sometimes kings had their thrones made of it, or panelled their rooms with it. It was used too in carving little figures and models.
1 Kings 22. 39; Psalm 45. 8.

J JABBOK. One of the streams that flows into the River Jordan about twenty miles north of the Dead Sea. Jacob passed over this stream with his family on the night that God spoke to him. *Genesis 32. 22.*

JABESH-GILEAD. The men of Jabesh-Gilead, a small town on the eastern side of the River Jordan, were threatened by the fierce Ammonite fighters. They appealed to Saul for help and he came and fought the Ammonites and saved the town. The townsmen never forgot this. When King Saul himself was killed in the battle of Gilboa they came by night and secured his body and reverently buried it in their own town. *1 Samuel 11. 1–11; 31. 11–13.*

JACOB (see also *Israel*).   According to the story in the Book of Genesis Jacob was born holding the heel of his twin-brother Esau. To the Biblical writer the name means 'he clutched'. He envied Esau because he was the elder and secured Esau's birthright by giving him a meal when he was hungry. He got the blessing of Isaac their father, but had to flee from home because of the trouble he had caused. In his wanderings God spoke to him through various experiences. Jacob dreamed that he saw a ladder stretching up from earth to heaven and leading into the presence of God. God promised that Jacob should become the father of a great people. At every stage of his life Jacob—with all his faults—remembered to worship God. He erected many places of worship. From his twelve sons came the people of Israel. Like Jacob they often disobeyed God but always returned in spirit to worship him. *Genesis 28. 11–22.*

JAEL.   The wife of Heber who killed the great soldier Sisera. When the Israelites defeated Sisera's Canaanites Jael invited the tired and defeated general into her tent. She gave him milk to drink and put him to rest. Jael's people were neutral and Sisera should have been safe in her home. In his sleep she drove a tent-peg into his head and killed him.   *Judges 4. 17–22.*

JAIRUS.   This is a name that is remembered because of what Jesus did in Jairus' home in Capernaum. He was a ruler of the synagogue and his little daughter was very ill. He came to Jesus and asked for his help, and while Jesus was going to his house the news spread that the child had died. Why bother Jesus any more? But Jesus walked on to the house and there took the child by the hand and lifted her up, and immediately she walked again.   *Mark 5. 22–43.*

JAMES.   There are three men called James in the Gospels. One of them is the fisherman of Galilee, a son of Zebedee, who with his brother John was one of the twelve apostles. He, with John and Peter, was a very close friend of Jesus. Another apostle ('Son of Alphaeus') was also called James. The third James was the brother of Jesus— and became a leader of the church in Jerusalem. Thirty years after the crucifixion of Jesus he himself was stoned to death by the Jews.   *Matthew 4. 21; 10. 3; 13. 55.*

JAMES, EPISTLE OF.   This short letter of five chapters in the New Testament is not

Jacob dreamed that
there was a ladder
set up on earth
and the top of it
reached to heaven

a letter like Paul's letters. It is a kind of sermon delivered to Jews who had become Christians and had not fully made up their minds whether Jesus was the Messiah or not. Traditionally the book has been credited to James, the brother of Jesus, and thought to have been written about 25 years after Jesus rose from the dead. Scholars today are not sure about this. The writer speaks of the many virtues that Christians must have such

In Jairus' home Jesus took the child by the hand

as patience, humility, and self-control. They must demonstrate their faith with good works. It is very Jewish in its style of writing. But it offers a lot of sound Christian guidance to its readers. *Epistle of James.*

JAPHETH. One of the sons of Noah who with his wife entered the Ark and was saved from the great flood. Japheth's descendants are usually said to be the people who settled in the region between the Caspian Sea and the Black Sea, and in what is now Turkey. *Genesis 5. 32.*

JASON. A Christian Jew in the city of Salonika. Paul lived in his house. The Jewish mob raided the house. But they failed to capture Paul and took Jason to the courts and accused him of upsetting the peace of the city. They let him go after he had promised not to create an uproar. *Acts 17. 5–9.*

JASPER. Several precious stones of different colours were called jasper in the Bible. Nowadays it is a dark red stone. *Revelation 21. 18.*

JAVELIN. A lighter and shorter form of spear which could be carried easily slung across the back. *1 Samuel 19. 10.*

JEALOUS. In the Bible God is often described as a 'jealous' God. He alone is to be worshipped by Israel. He is their God. He expects his people to be faithful to him and not to run after other gods. *Exodus 20. 5.*

JEBUSITE. On the hills round Jerusalem lived the Jebusites, descendants of Canaan who was a grandson of Noah. They gave the name Jebus to Jerusalem. *Numbers 13. 29.*

JEDIDIAH. Another name for King Solomon meaning 'beloved of the Lord' given to him at his birth. *2 Samuel 12. 25.*

JEHOIACHIN (see also *Jehoiakim*). He succeeded his father Jehoiakim as king of Judah when he was only eight. He was a puppet of the Babylonian overlords and reigned for only three months (598–597

B.C.). He was then carried off to Babylon with his mother. *2 Chronicles 36. 9.*

JEHOIADA. A favourite name in the Old Testament. One of the most famous men to bear the name was the chief priest

JEHOVAH (see also *God*). The Old Testament writers often referred to God as 'Yahweh' which English Bibles translate as Jehovah, or Lord. It is a personal name for God. It shows that God had close personal

Jehoiada. He guided the reign of the young King Joash of Judah who was only seven when he became king in 837 B.C. He did many good things for God and the people and when he died he was given a royal burial. *2 Kings 11–12; 2 Chronicles 24. 15.*

JEHOIAKIM. A king of Judah for eleven years (609–598 B.C.). In his reign Nebuchadnezzar won control of the kingdom and

links with the Hebrew people. He belonged to them. He was their own God.
Isaiah 12. 2.

Failing to capture Paul the mob caught Jason

JEHU. For twenty-seven years (842–815 B.C.) Jehu reigned over Israel. He won his way to power by many bloodthirsty deeds. He was famous as a reckless driver of chariots. He threw out all the 'foreign gods' in Israel, but yet was not a faithful follower

carried off many Jews as prisoners and one of them was the king himself.
2 Kings 23. 36–37; 24. 1–6.

JEHOSHAPHAT. One of the good kings of Judah who reigned from 873–849 B.C. He got rid of many pagan forms of worship, and made his people follow the laws of God as given to Moses. He organized the legal system of Judah and is remembered in Jewish history as one who served God and cared for his people. *2 Chronicles 19.*

of the one true God of Israel. Under him Israel did not prosper. *2 Kings 9. 17ff.*

JEPHTHAH. Jephthah was a judge in the days when the people of Israel were governed by judges, more than a thousand years before Jesus came. The Israelites had to defend themselves against the Ammonites. After the defeat of the Ammonites Jephthah vowed that he would offer as a sacrifice the first person who met him on his return. The first person was his only

Jehu the son of Nimshi drives furiously

77

daughter! Jephthah kept his vow. The women of Israel every year remembered the obedience of father and daughter.
Judges 11. 34–40.

JEREMIAH, BOOK OF. A great prophet of the Old Testament. He worked in the years between 640 B.C. and 587 B.C. Five kings of Judah reigned during this period, while the empires of Assyria, Egypt and Babylon struggled for the mastery of the land. From the heart of Judah Jeremiah spoke about God. He reminded kings and emperors that it is God who created the world and God who governs it. He spoke of God's judgment on the world. But at the same time he spoke of religion as being a very personal relation between God and Man. You could not be truly religious unless you were religious at heart. God looked not on the outward things but on the inner life. Jeremiah looked forward to the day when God would make this clear in someone who would come from God himself. He looked forward to the coming of Jesus Christ and spoke of the 'new covenant' between God and Israel.
Book of Jeremiah.

JERICHO. No city in the Bible is more famous than Jericho. But its story goes back a long way before Bible times as far as 8000 years before Jesus came. The site of the old Jericho lies about ten miles north-west of where the River Jordan empties into the Dead Sea. Modern Jericho is a mile away and about seventeen miles north-east of Jerusalem. When Joshua and his invading army came to Jericho the city had two parallel walls, the inner one twelve feet, and the outer one six feet thick. Jericho lies in an earthquake area, and many scholars believe that it was an earthquake which caused the walls of Jericho to fall miraculously to Joshua's army. Joshua then destroyed the city and laid a curse on it. For hundreds of years no one lived there. But just before Jesus came King Herod built a palace amongst the Jericho palm groves and a town grew up there, and Jericho became a favourite place to visit.
Joshua 6; Luke 10. 30.

JEROBOAM. The first king of Israel, who reigned for 22 years from 922–901 B.C., was called Jeroboam, and then from 786 B.C. Jeroboam II reigned for forty years. Both were vigorous rulers who made Israel (the northern part of the divided kingdom of which Judah was the southern) respected by other nations.
1 Kings 12. 20; 2 Kings 14. 23–27.

JERUSALEM. The story of Jerusalem goes back two thousand years before Christ. It is set among the hills of Judah, thirty miles from the Mediterranean Sea and twenty miles from the Dead Sea. It is sometimes

Jesus in Jerusalem—follow the arrows from the Upper Room to Golgotha

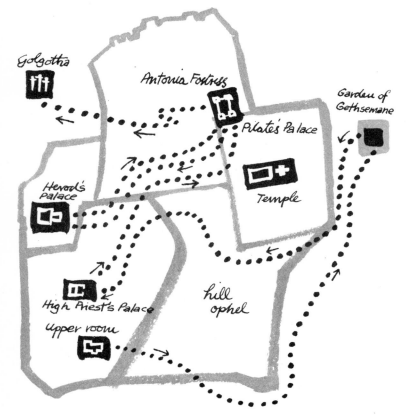

Golgotha

Antonia Fortress

Garden of Gethsemane

Pilate's Palace

Temple

Herod's Palace

High Priest's Palace

hill ophel

Upper room

referred to as *Salem* which means 'peace'. David captured the city from the Jebusites and made it his capital. To the Jews it was a most holy place because it contained the Temple. David and Solomon were the two great kings who built some of the city's fine buildings and strengthened the walls. Nebuchadnezzar of Babylon destroyed the city and the Temple in 587 B.C. Then the Jews came back and re-built the Temple and the walls. After that came Egyptians, Syrians, Romans, Arabs and Turks, who in turn conquered Jerusalem. Again and again the Jews revolted against their conquerors. In the days of Jesus the Romans were masters of Jerusalem but the Jews had freedom of worship in the Temple and regarded Jerusalem as their own city. *Psalm 122; Luke 21. 20ff.*

JESSE (see also *David*). The father of David, who lived on his farm in Bethlehem. He had eight sons but the Bible only names seven of them. *1 Chronicles 2. 13–15.*

JESUS CHRIST (see also *Gospel*). The Bible is about God and his Eternal Son Jesus Christ. The Old Testament looks towards the coming of Jesus, and the New Testament describes this great event. Jesus was born into an ordinary Jewish family, and grew up in a humble home with his mother, Mary, his earthly father Joseph and several younger brothers and sisters. He knew the Old Testament well, and was brought up as a Jewish boy. He worked with Joseph in the family carpenter's shop in Nazareth. Jesus was about thirty years old when he left Nazareth to start his teaching and preaching. In the villages of Galilee he showed his power to heal people. He called twelve men to be with him, and trained them as his disciples. They gradually came to believe that he was 'Christ' the Messiah—the One sent by God to save his people. His teachings brought much opposition from official religious leaders of the

day. They finally had Jesus arrested and crucified. He died and was buried. But he rose from the dead and showed himself alive to his disciples over a period of forty days. His disciples believed that he was the Son of God. When he ascended to be with his Father in heaven they worshipped him. Jesus lived a perfect human life on earth. But he was also divine—God in human form. All who have faith in him, in his life,

Jesus in Galilee— where he first called men to follow him

his death on the Cross, and his resurrection from the dead, are saved from the old life of sin to the new life in God's kingdom. *The Bible.*

JETHRO. The name of Moses' father-in-law. Moses was shepherding Jethro's sheep when God appeared to him in the wilderness of Sinai. *Exodus 3. 1.*

JEWS (see also *Gentiles*). Originally the name meant someone who belonged to the land of Judah. But by the time of Jesus Jews had spread to many other parts of Palestine, and later were found in nearly every part of the Roman Empire. The name was gradually used to cover all people who traced their descent to Jacob (Israel), or were called Hebrews. The Jews were a very religious people worshipping the one true God according to the laws of Moses. They kept their customs and worship wherever they went, which made them live very separately from other peoples. Jesus himself was a Jew brought up in a Jewish home. There he was trained in the traditions of the

Job said,
'How long will
you torment me,
and break me in
pieces with words?'

Jews. He was taught the Jewish 'Bible' which is the Old Testament, and he preached in the Jewish synagogues.
Nehemiah 1; John 18. 20–40; Romans 3. 29.

JEZEBEL (see also *Ahab* and *Elijah*). One of the wicked but clever women of the Old Testament. The wife of King Ahab, she believed in and worshipped her own gods (*baal*). She maintained over four hundred priests and expected her gods to be equal to the one true God of Israel. Elijah challenged these priests on Mount Carmel and won a great victory over them. *1 Kings 21.*

JEZREEL. A town, and a valley which slopes down towards the River Jordan with Galilee to the north and Mount Gilboa to the south. With the little River Jalud flowing down it Jezreel is a rich, fertile valley, and a route from the Jordan to the coast. It means 'God will sow', a reminder of the good crops grown in the valley. *Judges 6. 33.*

JOAB. A nephew of King David who fought in his army and became commander-in-chief. He was ambitious, cruel and selfish. He did many evil deeds hoping to please David. One of them was the killing of Absalom, David's rebel son. He later plotted against King Solomon and was killed by the king's orders.
2 Samuel 18. 14; 1 Kings 2. 28ff.

JOASH. Three men of note in the Old Testament are called by this name. One was the father of Gideon; the second Joash was king of Judah (837–800 B.C.) who did 'that which was right in the sight of God'; the third Joash was king of Israel (801–786 B.C.) and friend of Elisha the prophet.
Judges 6. 11; 2 Kings 12. 1–3; 13. 14.

JOB, BOOK OF JOB. According to tradition Job was a prosperous landowner who lived far across the Jordan in the land of Uz. He had much wealth in cattle and crops and a large family of ten children. But he fell ill and all his friends and family said it was due to his own faults—his own sins. They threw him out of the town and Job sat in misery on a dunghill. He was visited by three friends who did not give him much comfort. Job found the way out of his troubles by turning again to God in repentance and hope.

The Book of Job is the story of Job's sufferings and his recovery. It is really a long poem written about five hundred years before Christ. The writer is unknown. The book tells a very human story. Job was a good man and worshipped God and obeyed him in his life. He wondered why God allowed all these sufferings to come upon him. At last he realized that God was greater and more wonderful than himself and that God saw beyond what Job saw and that he knew best. *Book of Job.*

JOEL. Joel's prophecy in the Old Testament, is written in the form of poetry in three short chapters. It is the cry of a prophet in the land of Judah about a great plague of locusts. This plague is a sign of God's anger. He calls the people to repent. God will then send his Spirit amongst men, and there will be rejoicing and gladness once more in the earth. The book was written about four hundred years before Christ. *Book of Joel.*

JOHN, THE APOSTLE. 'One of his disciples, whom Jesus loved.' That is the description given in John's Gospel of a disciple. Which one? It is usually thought to be the apostle John, the fisherman son of a fisherman father Zebedee. With his brother James he followed Jesus in Galilee. It may have been that he was cousin to Jesus for it is thought that their mothers, Salome and Mary, were sisters. He was with Jesus on many important occasions. At the crucifixion Jesus asked John to look after his mother. John lived on in Jerusalem and became a leader of the Christian church there, but then he disappeared. Some think

he was banished to the island of Patmos and there wrote the Book of Revelation.
Matthew 4. 21; Revelation 1.

JOHN, THE BAPTIST. 'Now John was clothed with camel's hair, and had a leather girdle around his waist, and ate locusts and wild honey.' That is how Mark describes the man who preached to the people of Judaea, and lived in the wild country outside Jerusalem. Crowds came to hear him preach and his message always was, 'Repent and be baptized.' Jesus himself came to

**Destructive—
the locust is also
edible as
John the Baptist
discovered**

John to be baptized. John thought of himself as one who prepared the way for Jesus. He was a fearless preacher. He preached against King Herod marrying his brother's wife Herodias. This angered Herodias who prompted her daughter—as a favour from the king—to ask for John's death. *Mark 1. 4 ff; 6. 25 ff.*

JOHN, EPISTLES OF. Three short letters at the end of the Bible are called the first, second and third letters of John. They were written about seventy years after the resurrection of Jesus. They were written to warn Christians against various false teachings which many Christians were listening to. The writer warns his readers not to be deceived but to make sure that everything they were asked to believe really did come from the teaching of Jesus. He may have written the Gospel of John. *Epistles of John.*

JOHN, GOSPEL OF (see also *Gospels*). The Gospel of John is one of the most profound books in the Bible. The writer, who may have been John the apostle, sets out to tell the story of Jesus Christ. He looks back after many years on the wonderful events of Christ's life on earth. He looks at Jesus in many different ways. He speaks of him as the Lamb of God, the Bread of Life, the True Vine, the Light of this World, and as Saviour of the World. He weaves all these various pictures of Jesus into one wonderful portrait. By the time this Gospel was written many people had heard about Jesus—Greeks as well as Jews. The writer keeps them all in mind. He paints a portrait of Jesus so that every one could be attracted to him, and believe in him. He is eager that the whole world should know about Jesus, who did so many things 'that the world itself could not contain the books that would be written.'
Gospel of John.

JONAH. This prophecy was preached in Israel about eight hundred years before Jesus. Jonah is the hero of the book. In the story related in the book Jonah is told by God to go and preach in the wicked city of Nineveh, but he disobeys God and sails on a ship in the opposite direction. A storm arises and in the storm the sailors throw Jonah overboard. He is then swallowed by a big fish who carries Jonah inside its belly and casts him up safely on shore. After all this Jonah goes to Nineveh and preaches to the sinful city. His adventure taught him that God's love covers all kinds of people, and not the Jews alone. Through this parable the people of Israel were taught that their God was the God of the whole human race; a truth that they took a long time to learn.
Book of Jonah.

JONATHAN. The eldest son of King Saul who became the close friend of David.

After David's successful fight against the giant Goliath, Jonathan took his own robe and put it on the young hero. He gave him his sword, his bow and his girdle and was proud to call David his friend. When Saul planned to kill David Jonathan warned him. He arranged for David to escape from his father's clutches, and was ready to take the blame to himself. He died with his father in the Battle of Gilboa in 1000 B.C. David sang for the two men a song of grief and thanksgiving which is one of the loveliest songs in the Bible. *2 Samuel 1. 19–27.*

JOPPA. A sea-port on the coast of Israel now called Jaffa and joined to Tel Aviv. In the story of Jonah, Joppa is the place Jonah set sail from. It was in Joppa that Peter saw his vision of the great sheet in which all the animals of the world had a place—a reminder to Peter that God created them all, and that he should despise none of God's creation. *Acts 11. 5ff.*

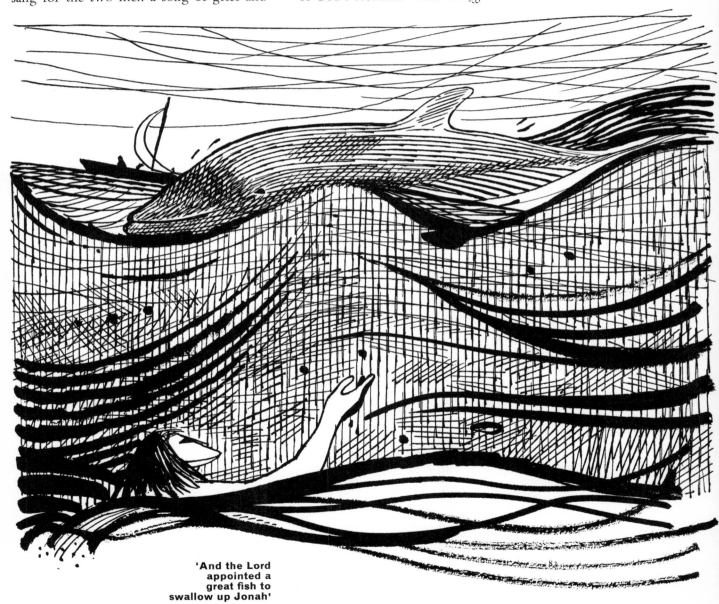

'And the Lord appointed a great fish to swallow up Jonah'

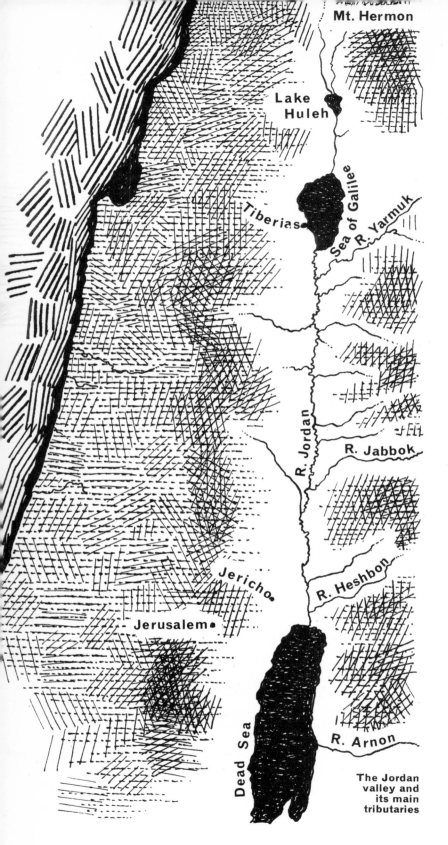

The Jordan valley and its main tributaries

JORDAN. The River Jordan is the most famous river mentioned in the Bible. It was the river that Jesus knew as a young man, and he was baptized in it by John the Baptist. Its name means the 'descender' and that is a good name for it. It descends from the foothills round Mount Hermon, down through the Sea of Galilee dropping steeply through its deep trench. By the time it reaches the north end of the Dead Sea, where it finally loses itself in the salt water, it is 1290 feet below sea-level. The Jordan valley is called a 'rift valley', and of its kind is the deepest in the world. The river itself is only 75 miles long but in its wild curves it covers nearly twice that length.
Joshua 3. 8ff; Matthew 3. 13ff.

JOSEPH. Joseph was the favourite son of Jacob. His father gave him presents that made his brothers envious. One day he gave him a beautiful coat of many colours. When they saw him in this his brothers planned to kill him. But instead they put him into a deep pit, and then sold him to some travelling merchants, who in turn sold Joseph as a 'slave' in Egypt. There he suffered imprisonment for his loyalty to his master Potiphar. He was brought out of prison to interpret Pharaoh's dreams and became a favourite of Pharaoh, who listened to his advice about the supplies of food in Egypt. When a group of Hebrews came into Egypt looking for food in a time of famine Joseph recognized his brothers of long ago—but they did not know him. Joseph treated them kindly, gave them supplies of grain to take home to his old father, and gave them back their money too. Jacob and his sons then came to live in Egypt and were very proud to be known as relations of Joseph. The Joseph story shows God's special link with the family of Jacob and his care for their welfare.

Joseph is also the name of the husband of Mary, the mother of Jesus. He acted as father to Jesus doing all the things that a

Jewish father did for his son. It is likely that Joseph died early in life as there is no mention of him in the Bible when Jesus himself was a grown man.
Genesis 37; 39–50; Matthew 1. 18ff.

JOSHUA. The leader of the people of Israel into the Promised Land. He was chosen by Moses as his personal assistant. Just before they crossed the River Jordan into the Promised Land Joshua stood before all the people and was appointed their leader by Moses. He was then about seventy years old. Joshua led the people across the River Jordan to capture the first cities. He planned the division of the country according to the tribes. He was over a hundred years old when he died. In his old age he challenged the people to choose God rather than the idols of the land they had conquered. *Numbers 27. 18–23; Joshua 4; 24.*

JOSHUA, BOOK OF. This book in the Bible is called the 'Book of Joshua' because it tells the story of how Joshua led the people of Israel into the land of Canaan, or the Promised Land, after their years of wandering across the wilderness from Egypt. It describes the battles they fought and gives the names of the many tribes they conquered. It describes how the land was divided up amongst the Israelites and the struggles the people had to keep true to God, for they were often tempted to follow the religious ways of their new country. The writer of the Book of Joshua describes the mighty acts of God in establishing the children of Israel in the Promised Land, and of God's ways with them. It is thought that the writers of the Book of Deuteronomy also wrote the Book of Joshua.
Book of Joshua.

JOSIAH. The young king of Judah who reigned for thirty years (640–609 B.C.). He was a good king. During his reign the 'book of the law', the Book of Deuteronomy, was discovered in the Temple. From the read-ing of the book Josiah learned of the laws of God that had been given to his fore-fathers. He saw that many things were wrong in the national life and started to clean up the land. Heathen worship was abolished, and the people were encouraged to worship the one true God. Josiah was

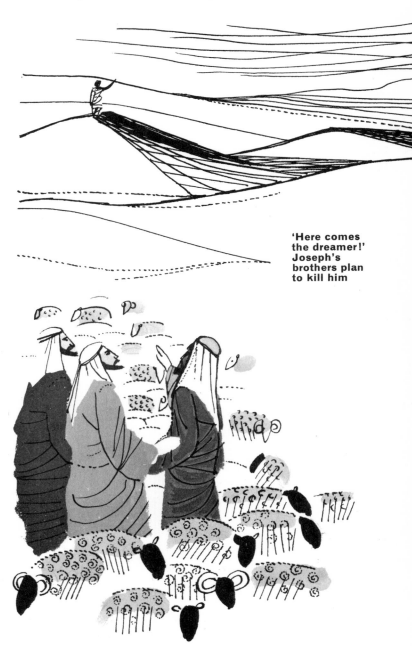

'Here comes the dreamer!' Joseph's brothers plan to kill him

killed in battle against the invading Egyptians. *2 Kings 22. 1-2; 23. 1-30.*

JUBILEE, YEAR OF. The people of the Old Testament had a tradition allowing the land 'to rest' every seven years. After all the ploughing and tilling the land grew tired and for a year it rested. Every fifty years this idea was then supposed to be extended to living people. Debts could then be forgiven, slaves released, and property given back to its original owners. It was called a Jubilee Year—a year of thanksgiving to God for all his goodness.
Leviticus 25. 8-12.

JUDAH, JUDAEA. Judah was the fourth son of Jacob, and father of the tribe of Judah which settled in the southern hilly area of the Promised Land with Hebron as their chief town. It became a separate kingdom like the kingdom of Israel to the north. This little land of farms and small towns lay on the route between Egypt and the north. It was often attacked and invaded. Nebuchadnezzar took off many of its people to Babylon 598-587 B.C. In the days of Jesus it was a province of the Roman Empire. The name 'Judah' stands for 'Jew'.
Genesis 29. 35; Matthew 2. 6.

JUDAS ISCARIOT. The disciple of Jesus who betrayed him to the Jewish authorities came from 'Kerioth' or 'Iscarioth' near the town of Hebron in Judah. He looked after the money of the little group of Jesus' friends. It was partly his love of money that led him to make a bargain to betray Jesus for 'thirty pieces of silver'. But it may be that he was disappointed in Jesus and the message he preached. He was afterwards very sorry for what he did, and killed himself. *Matthew 26. 14-16, 47-50.*

JUDE, LETTER OF. This writing is the last 'book' but one in the Bible. It may have been written by Jude (or Judas) who was one of the brothers of Jesus. It was probably sent round amongst Christians, many years

Ark over Jordan—the climax of Joshua's campaign

after the resurrection of Christ, to warn them against false teaching. False teachers were going about amongst the churches and were spreading mis-statements on the faith. The writer encourages his readers to believe only in Christ and to help those in doubt. *Letter of Jude.*

JUDGES, BOOK OF. The Book of Judges, the seventh book in the Bible, tells the story of life in Palestine twelve hundred years before Jesus came. Those were the days when the people of Israel were settling into their new home. There was much warfare and conflict with their new neighbours. So 'judges' were appointed to go amongst the people to settle these quarrels and to 'govern' the country. The book describes how the people of Israel had to fight hard to keep their new home and it has adventurous stories such as those of Gideon, Deborah and Samson who were amongst the 'judges'. The 'judges' helped to keep up the people's spirits, always reminding them of their special links with the one true God. They could only conquer their enemies by remaining true to God. *Book of Judges.*

JUDGMENT HALL. The Jewish priests brought Jesus to the Roman governor Pilate at his house called the Praetorium or Judgment Hall. The priests stood outside the house but Pilate took Jesus inside to talk with him privately. *John 18. 28–33.*

K **KADESH.** Kadesh was on the route of the Israelites across the Sinai wilderness. It had water, grass for cattle and it was near the borders of the Promised Land in the north-east of the Sinai peninsula. It was there that Moses learned that he would not lead the people into their new home. From there too he sent out the spies into the land of Canaan. *Numbers 20. 1–13.*

KEDAR. Kedar was one of the sons of Ishmael and his descendants were famous in Bible times for their beautiful black tents. They moved around with their sheep pitching their black tents wherever the grazing was good. The tents when grouped together looked like complete villages. *Isaiah 42. 11.*

KERIOTH. A town in the extreme south of Judah mentioned in the long list of places which the tribe of Judah took over in the Promised Land. *Joshua 15. 25.*

KETURAH. Abraham's second wife, after the death of Sarah, and the mother of six of his sons. *Genesis 25. 1–4.*

KEY. Only once in the Bible is the word 'key' mentioned as a key to open a door. The other seven times it is used as a word to describe power or authority. *Judges 3. 25; Revelation 3. 7.*

Kidron—
wild valley
outside
Jerusalem

KIDRON. On the north side of Jerusalem runs a deep valley called Kidron. In the rainy season a 'brook', or stream, runs down it. Jesus often crossed the valley to his favourite Garden of Gethsemane. It was the way of escape from Jerusalem that David used in fleeing from his son Absalom.
2 Samuel 15. 23; John 18. 1.

KING. The word 'king' is mentioned over four hundred times in the Bible. It probably means to 'possess'. Jesus thought of himself as 'King' but his 'kingdom' was not of the earthly kind but a 'kingdom' in men's hearts. *John 18. 37.*

KINGDOM OF GOD. 'Seek ye the kingdom.' That phrase often comes in the Gospels in the New Testament for it was used by Jesus to describe his way of life. Sometimes he called it 'kingdom of heaven' or 'kingdom of God'. He thought of his kingdom as a reign of peace and love for all men on earth. He also thought of it as the 'kingdom' which would come when this world had passed away. He thought too of the church as the company of people who prepared the way for the coming of the kingdom. The members of his church were to show by the way they lived what the kingdom would be like.
Matthew 13; John 18. 36.

KINGS, BOOKS OF. Two books in the Old Testament are called the First and Second Books of Kings. They tell the story of four hundred years of the kings of Israel and Judah beginning at the end of David's reign. The story finishes about five hundred years before Jesus came. The main aim of the writer is to show how God dealt with his people through the various events of history. The writer judges the various kings by how they behaved towards God. He is concerned chiefly with how they conduct themselves as worshippers of the one true God. There are some wonderful stories in the Books of Kings about many fine and noble people. But there are others that tell of the bad side of the kings and of the evil they did. The two books are very human and tell of the ways of God with men.
First and Second Books of Kings.

KISH. Five men in the Old Testament are called Kish: one of them is the father of King Saul. *1 Samuel 9. 1.*

KISHON. A river that flows into the Mediterranean Sea near Mount Carmel. It was on the banks of the Kishon that the Israelites won a big battle over the Syrians. The river overflowed its banks and flooded the plain and made the land too soft for the Syrian chariots, which got stuck in the mud.
Judges 4 and 5.

KISS. In Bible times it was a common habit to greet anyone coming into a house

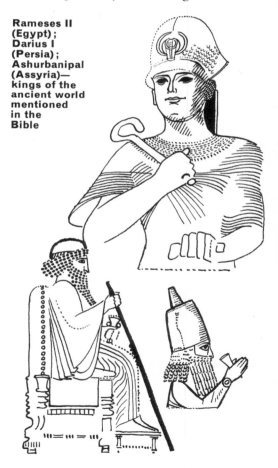

Rameses II (Egypt); Darius I (Persia); Ashurbanipal (Assyria)— kings of the ancient world mentioned in the Bible

Kneading trough for the kitchen

with a kiss. It was part of the hospitality custom. After the kiss came the washing of the dusty feet. In the early days of the Christian church it was sometimes the custom to give a 'holy kiss' as a sign of Christian love.
Genesis 29. 11; Romans 16. 16.

KNEADING TROUGH. Most homes of the Bible had a kneading trough for the making of dough. The flour, water, salt and a little leaven were pounded, or kneaded, together by hand before the bread, or cake, was put over the fire for baking. The trough was made of pottery or wood. *Exodus 12. 34.*

KNEE, KNEEL. In the New Testament to 'kneel' means to bow, or worship, or give respect. But in the Old Testament 'feeble knees' or 'to shake at the knees' means to be afraid. *Isaiah 35. 3; Mark 1. 40.*

KNIFE. This word comes often in the Old Testament. A knife was sometimes made of flint and shaped like a dagger, or short sword, such as the one Abraham took to kill Isaac. Later knives were made of copper, bronze or iron. *Genesis 22. 6.*

L **LABAN.** The father of Leah and Rachel, who lived in Haran: a man with many flocks and herds. He demanded from Jacob work for seven years before Rachel could be his wife, and then another seven years' work after that, and more work to acquire his own flocks. Jacob felt that he had been treated harshly, and fled with his family and possessions. Laban chased after him, and the two men then made an agreement to live in peace. *Genesis 31.*

Knives—of flint and metal—sometimes a short sword

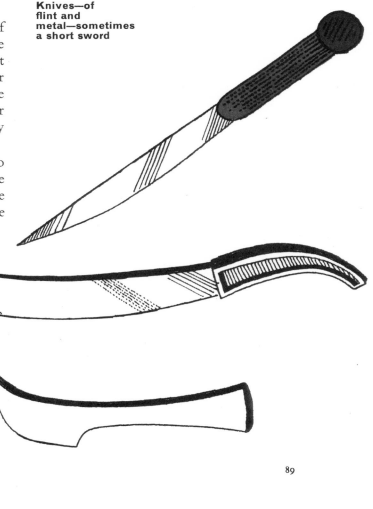

89

LACHISH. 'And Joshua passed to Lachish, and laid siege to it and assaulted it.' In these words the Book of Joshua records the capture of this important city which guarded the main road leading up to Jerusalem. Joshua burned the city and many traces of burning have been found by digging into the site of Lachish. The city was later rebuilt by the people of Judah with towers, gateways and high walls. They made a deep well too, to make sure of plenty of water. Later still, the Assyrians captured the city and carried off its people to Nineveh. By the time of Jesus Lachish was a heap of ruins. *Joshua 10. 31–34.*

LAMENTATIONS, THE. Perhaps the saddest book in the Bible. It records how the people of Judah mourned the destruction of the Temple and of Jerusalem. It is written in the form of a funeral poem or a dirge. When King Nebuchadnezzar of Babylon captured Jerusalem in 597 B.C., he carried off hundreds of Jews with him. They knew that they had not kept their promises to God and had done wrong. So the Book of Lamentations describes their repentance. In their sadness the Jewish people look forward to better times. Some people think that Jeremiah wrote the book as it is very much like his own. *The Lamentations.*

LAMB OF GOD. This is a phrase that is used twice in the New Testament to describe Jesus. It is spoken by John the Baptist about Jesus. John thought of Jesus as one who would sacrifice himself for the sake of those he loved. He thought of him as 'the lamb' which he had often seen sacrificed in the worship of the Temple.
John 1. 29, 36.

LAMECH. Lamech, which means 'a strong, young man', was a descendant of Cain. One of his sons was Tubal-cain, the first man to make things in metal, in iron and bronze. Lamech was proud and cruel and boasted that he had killed a man.
Genesis 4. 19–24.

LAMP (see also *Candle*). The simple, common lamp of Bible times was an open bowl with a wick floating in the oil. Ten young girls once took their lamps to a wedding party, said Jesus, to light the bridegroom's way to the marriage feast. At midnight the bridegroom arrived and the girls rushed to fill their lamps with oil. Five of them had

A lamp without oil is useless

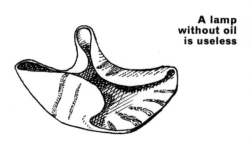

90

plenty of oil and lit the wicks of their lamps lying in their bowls of oil. But the other five ran out of oil and rushed out to buy more. While they were gone the bridegroom entered the house and the door was shut. This story about being ready with well-supplied lamps was told to remind people to be ready for the coming of God's kingdom. *Matthew 25. 1–11.*

LANTERN. On the night Jesus was arrested in the Garden of Gethsemane the soldiers carried lanterns. This is the only time a lantern is mentioned in the Bible. Perhaps it was just a covered lamp. *John 18. 3.*

LAODICEA. The Christians who lived in

'For these things I weep; my eyes flow with tears; my children are desolate, for the enemy has prevailed' (Lamentations)

this city, in what is now the country of Turkey, did not have a very good name. They were said to be 'lukewarm', neither 'hot' nor 'cold'. Their wealth and their comfort made them lazy in mind and body. *Revelation 3. 14–22.*

LATCHET (see also *Footwashing, Sandal*). Most people in Bible times wore sandals which were tied on to the feet by a leather thong called a 'latchet'. It was the task of an under-servant in a big household to untie the latchets of the sandals. John the Baptist said he was not fit to untie the latchet of Jesus' sandals. *Mark 1. 7.*

LAVER. A big basin or trough made of bronze or copper for the priests to wash their feet and hands in during worship in the Temple. *Exodus 30. 17–21.*

LAW (see also *Deuteronomy*). The word 'law' appears over two hundred times in the Old Testament. It is a word that is very precious to the Hebrew people. All through their history from the time of Moses they collected God's commandments about how they should live and worship. These were put down in writing on parchment scrolls and kept in the Temple and read at the time of worship. The chief books of 'the law' are the first five books in the Bible. The Jews look on them with very great respect, and try to carry out every letter of the law they lay down. Jesus too respected the Jewish law. But he said that the greatest commandment was to 'love your God with

Lazarus at the gate asked for the rich man's crumbs

all your heart', and the second is 'love your neighbour as yourself'.
Exodus 24. 12; Matthew 22. 34–40.

LAWYERS. The lawyers in the time of Jesus were men skilled in the exact observances of the Jewish law. They were always on the watch to see what Jesus would say and do. For instance, according to the law no one must work on the Sabbath. But Jesus once healed a sick man on the Sabbath and then asked the lawyers whether he did right. Had he broken the law by working? He also asked them if one of them had a donkey which fell into a pit on the Sabbath would he not pull him out? The clever lawyers had no answer to this question. It was more important, in the eyes of Jesus, to be loving and helpful than to keep the exact letter of the law. *Luke 14. 1–6.*

LAZARUS AND THE RICH MAN. A certain rich man (sometimes called *Dives*), said Jesus, always refused to help the poor man Lazarus who sat begging at his gate. He had plenty of money and food but never shared them with the beggar. They both died. Lazarus went to 'heaven' and Dives to 'hell'. In his torment Dives called out for Lazarus to give him a cooling drink. But Abraham, who was caring for Lazarus, refused to send him relief because in his life-time he had not cared for others, but enjoyed his own comfort in a selfish manner. *Luke 16. 19–31.*

LAZARUS OF BETHANY. In the home that Jesus loved to go to in Bethany lived two sisters, Mary and Martha, and their brother Lazarus. Lazarus became ill and died. John tells how Jesus came to the home and insisted on going to the cave in which he was buried. In a loud voice he cried 'Lazarus come out' and the man got up and came out, with his hands and feet in bandages and his face covered with a cloth. *John 11. 17–44.*

LEAH. The elder daughter of Laban, and one of the wives of Jacob. She had six sons —Reuben, Simeon, Levi, Judah, Issachar, Zebulun—fathers of six tribes of Israel. *Genesis 29–30.*

LEAVEN (see also *Bread*). Leaven is the 'yeast' that stirs up the dough to become good bread. Flour and water are mixed and allowed to stand until sour. Then leaven is kneaded in with the new dough. Jesus said that a woman once put leaven in with a supply of meal until the whole of it was leavened. That was how his kingdom would work, he said. His followers were to be like leaven, working quietly inside the whole lump of dough until it became good wholesome bread.
Matthew 13. 33; 1 Corinthians 5. 6–8.

LEBANON. Lebanon is the name of the country that borders on to Israel in the north. Its high mountains are snow-capped and it has great forests. In Bible times, Lebanon was famous as the land of great trees, especially the mighty cedars. It was a land of orchards and vineyards—a beautiful land when looked at from the more barren land of Palestine. *Psalm 92. 12.*

LEGION (see also *Gadarene*). A legion was a division of the Roman army numbering

Lebanon—where the stately cedars grow

93

6000 men. When Jesus cast out the mad spirits from the man in the Gadarene country, the spirits said they were 'Legion' meaning that there were many of them. *Luke 8. 30.*

LEPROSY. A skin disease which began with tiny white spots and often spread rapidly. In Bible times, a person suffering from leprosy was called a 'leper' and had to keep away from other people. Jesus once healed ten men suffering from this skin disease, but only one man came back to thank him—and he was a foreigner, a Samaritan. *Luke 17. 11–19.*

LEVI. The third son of Jacob and Leah and the father of the Israelite tribe of Levi. *Genesis 29. 34.*

LEVIATHAN. It may be a huge fish, a whale, a big monster of the sea, a crocodile. The Bible does not describe 'Leviathan' exactly. *Psalm 104. 26.*

LEVITICUS, BOOK OF. Leviticus is the third book in the Bible. It is all about the worship of the Jewish people and their way of life. It is full of instructions or laws about conduct, duty and obedience to God. It instructs the Jews in the regulations of the law about food, dress, and illness. It gives the laws of worship, and reminds the Jews that God thinks of them as a very holy people. The Jewish people thought of the book as one belonging particularly to their priests. It has many special instructions for the priest to observe.
Book of Leviticus.

LIBERTY. In Old Testament times people were often captured and taken away into slavery. The Jews themselves had once been slaves in Egypt. So the word 'liberty' was a very precious word. It meant 'freedom'. The great prophet Isaiah wrote a wonderful poem about liberty which the Jews loved to read. In the New Testament 'liberty' meant freedom from all the old, bad things of life. Jesus brought a new kind

On Mount Sinai Moses saw the lightning flash

of 'liberty'. He freed people from their sins. *Isaiah 61. 1; 2 Corinthians 3. 17.*

LIGHTNING. Thunder storms with lightning often happened in Bible times. When Moses went to the top of Mount Sinai he saw the lightning flash. When Jesus rose from the dead, the angel at the tomb was said to look like 'lightning'. The word is sometimes used to mean 'bright' or 'glistening'. *Exodus 19. 16; Matthew 28. 3.*

LILY, LILIES. 'Consider the lilies of the field.' Jesus must often have seen the lily growing in Galilee with its tall stem and beautiful white and pink flower. It may be that he was also referring to many other flowers of Galilee as well, such as anemone, iris, narcissus, hyacinth and cyclamen. They all grew naturally and beautifully, an example of God's care for all his creation. *Matthew 6. 28.*

LINEN (see also *Flax*). Linen was woven from the flax-plant. It was much used by Jewish priests, who dressed in linen. Fine linen was expensive and was always thought to be a beautiful gift to be used, or worn, only on special occasions. *Exodus 28. 39; Matthew 27. 59.*

LION. To people in the Bible the lion meant 'strength' and 'power'. The lion had its home in Palestine, and the Old Testament writers mention him over a hundred times. *Judges 14. 18; Revelation 10. 3.*

LION OF JUDAH. This is one of the titles that the writer of the Book of Revelation gives Christ. Like the people of Judah, who are compared to the lion, he is a conqueror. Today the Emperor of Ethiopia calls himself by this name. He believes that he is

The flowers of Galilee—Jesus never forgot their beauty

descended from the people of Judah of King Solomon's time. *Genesis 49. 9; Revelation 5. 5.*

LIZARD. Amongst the animals mentioned in the Book of Leviticus is the 'lizard'. It was one of the 'unclean' animals which Jews were ordered not to eat. More than forty different kinds of lizards are known in Palestine. Among the most common are the green lizard and the one that climbs up the wall. *Leviticus 11. 29–30.*

LOCUST. Like a grass-hopper the locust had long legs to hop. It flew in swarms and often settled on one spot and ate up all the green vegetation. It was a pest to farmers. But it had an agreeable flavour and the Jews were allowed to eat it. One of the plagues of Egypt was a plague of locusts. John the Baptist lived on locusts in the wilderness. *Exodus 10. 4–6; Leviticus 11. 22; Mark 1. 6.*

95

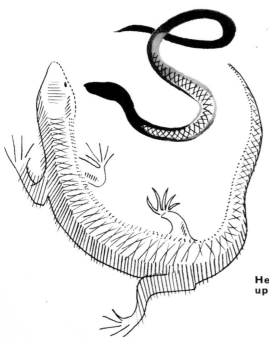

He even climbs up the wall

LOIS. Timothy's grandmother, and one who greatly influenced Paul's young friend. *2 Timothy 1. 5.*

LORD (see also *Jehovah*). The name 'Lord' is used in the Bible for anyone who is in authority. Rather than pronounce the name of God, the Jews spoke of 'the Lord'. So the name came to be used for Jesus. *Psalm 100; Matthew 26. 22.*

LORD'S DAY. This expression is found only in the Book of Revelation. By the time that book was written, Christians used to meet on the first day in each week for worship. It was natural that they should call it the 'Lord's Day'—the day on which they remembered the Lord Jesus Christ and his resurrection from the dead. The Romans used to have a day called 'Emperor's Day'. The Christians were sure that the authority of their Lord was greater than that of the emperor. *Revelation 1. 10.*

LORD'S PRAYER. 'Our Father which art in heaven.' This is the first sentence in the Lord's Prayer which Jesus gave to his disciples as the model for their prayers. Every sentence in it is a prayer by itself. The first three speak about God; the next three are about our own bodies and souls and what they need. We learn about our duty to forgive, and to ask for help in difficult times when we are tempted to sin. Finally we are told to look forward to the coming of Christ's kingdom. Jesus himself lived this prayer in his daily life. He said to his disciples 'when *ye* pray' say this— and then do it. *Matthew 6. 9–15.*

LORD'S SUPPER. Sometimes this meal which Jesus ate with his disciples on the night he was arrested is called the 'Last Supper'. Jesus often had an evening meal with his disciples but at this supper something different happened. As they were eating he took bread and passed it round amongst them and said, 'This is my body.'

He took a cup of wine and also passed it round and said, 'This is my blood.' He told his disciples to eat and drink in remembrance of him. Ever since then the Lord's Supper has been observed by the disciples of Jesus everywhere. They eat bread and drink wine in remembrance of him, and in thanksgiving for his life, death and resurrection. They 'feed on him' by faith. It is a 'holy communion' with Jesus. *Mark 14. 22–25.*

LOT (see also *Gomorrah*). Lot was the nephew of Abraham and went with him on the great journey towards the land of Palestine. When a quarrel arose between their various herdsmen Abraham and Lot agreed to part company. Lot chose the well-watered valley of the Jordan. There he

They cast lots

met the wicked people of the cities of Sodom and Gomorrah. When the two cities were destroyed Lot, his wife and his two daughters were rescued. But Lot's

Prodigal Son, Martha and Mary, the Widow of Nain, Dives and Lazarus, Zacchaeus, The Repentant Thief, the Good Samaritan and the Walk to Emmaus.

**He's alive!
Luke alone tells the
Prodigal's story**

wife looked back and the Bible says she was turned into a pillar of salt. *Genesis 19.*

LOTS. The casting of lots was a method often used in Bible times to make a decision. Stones with marks on them were shaken together in a vessel and then drawn out one by one. Each stone referred to a person who then made his choice. When Jesus died on the Cross, the soldiers cast lots for his clothes. *Numbers 26. 55; Matthew 27. 35.*

LUKE, GOSPEL OF (see also *Acts of Apostles*). Some people think Luke's Gospel is the most beautiful book in the Bible. It contains in detail the story of the birth of Jesus and many of his teachings. Some of the most unforgettable parables and stories of Jesus are told only by Luke. Only Luke's Gospel has the stories of the

Luke must have known someone who had been with Jesus and remembered what happened. Luke wrote about Jesus so that people who were not Jews might be attracted to him, and he continues the story in the Acts of the Apostles. *Gospel of Luke.*

LUKE, THE EVANGELIST. The man who wrote both the Gospel of Luke and the Acts of the Apostles. He was a well educated man, a medical doctor. He set out to write all he knew, and could find out, about Jesus, and to write it down in good order. He was a very close friend of Paul and travelled about with him. While in prison in Rome Paul wrote 'Only Luke is with me'. *Luke 1. 1–4; 2 Timothy 4. 11.*

LYCAONIA. A district of Asia Minor,

now in the country of Turkey, over which Paul travelled, and preached in the cities of Lycaonia such as Lystra and Derbe. *Acts 14. 6.*

LYDIA. Lydia lived in Philippi and was Paul's first convert in his European mission. She often gave Paul and his friends hospitality in her home; she was a business woman who traded in purple cloth. She had services in her home and by the riverside on the Sabbath. Like Paul, she was an Asiatic who became a Christian. *Acts 16. 14–15.*

LYSTRA (see also *Lois*). A small, obscure town on the high lands of what is now modern Turkey. Paul and Barnabas came there to preach, and out of their preaching a church grew. One of the families in the church was the family of Timothy who became such a close friend of Paul. *Acts 16. 1.*

M **MAACAH.** A personal name that is used a number of times in the Old Testament. Maacah was the mother of Absalom, King David's son. *2 Samuel 3. 3.*

MACEDONIA. 'Come over to Macedonia and help us.' That was the cry that Paul heard in a dream. He saw a man standing on the shore of Greece and calling to him to come across the sea and preach the Gospel in that part of the world. Paul was in Troas on the shores of Asia. Macedonia is the northern part of Greece, a land of farms and forests and rivers—the part of Europe first to hear the Christian Gospel. *Acts 16. 9.*

MACHIR. When King David was fighting against his son Absalom he was in the wilderness and was very hungry. Machir was one of the men who brought him food. He collected wheat and barley, beans and lentils, honey and curds—beds too for David and his followers to sleep on. The same name belongs to one of Joseph's grandsons in Egypt. *Genesis 50. 23; 2 Samuel 17. 27–29.*

Peter drew his sword to defend Jesus and wounded Malchus

MAGDALA, MAGDALENE. Magdala was a town on the western shore of the Sea of Galilee not far from Tiberias. Sometimes it is spelled Magadan. This was the home of Mary Magdalene who was healed by Jesus. She was one of the three women who came to the tomb of Jesus on the morning of the resurrection. While she stood crying at the entrance of the tomb Jesus himself appeared and spoke to her. Then she ran to tell the good news to his disciples. *Matthew 15. 39; John 20. 1–18.*

MAGICIANS, MAGI. The Bible uses these words to mean 'wise men'—those who know the hidden meaning of wonders that appear in the earth and the sky. 'Wise Men' had been following a very bright star across the desert country and found it led them to Bethlehem in Judaea. There they discovered the new born baby—Jesus Christ. They presented him with gifts and went away to their distant homes. They were glad to have seen him whose coming had been so long expected by the Jews. But they themselves were not Jews. They believed that Jesus had come to be the great star of light for all the world. *Daniel 2. 2; Matthew 2. 1–12.*

MAGNIFY. Mary, the mother of Jesus, spoke a lovely poem of praise to God when she heard the news that she was to be the mother of Jesus. 'My soul doth magnify the Lord', she said, and her poem is called the Magnificat—a poem that shows the greatness and the glory of God. *Luke 1. 46–55.*

MAHANAIM. A place in the land of Gilead, across the Jordan, where Jacob met the angels of God. *Genesis 32. 1–2.*

MAKKEDAH. One of the cities captured by Joshua when he entered the Promised Land. *Joshua 10. 28.*

MALACHI. This prophecy in the Old Testament has four short chapters. It was probably written nearly five hundred years

before Jesus came. It describes how the Jews are living again in Jerusalem after their exile. But Malachi, which means 'my messenger', warns the people of their sins. They forget to worship God and they run after 'false Gods' and 'heathen worship'. They are careless in morals and fail to give their best to God. But the prophet is glad that there are some people who remember God and their duty to him.

Book of Malachi.

MALCHUS. The servants of the high priest went to arrest Jesus in the Garden of Gethsemane. One of them was called Malchus. When Peter who was with Jesus saw that they were taking Jesus away he became angry and pulled out a short sword and cut off the ear of Malchus. But Jesus warned him that no good could come from using a sword in that way. He touched the ear and healed it.   *John 18. 10.*

MAMMON.   This word comes twice in the

The star went before them to Bethlehem

Bible and means 'wealth' or 'profit'. It is used to describe someone who is greedy about money, or who gets money in dishonest ways. Jesus said that you cannot serve God and Mammon at the same time. *Matthew 6. 24; Luke 16. 13.*

MAMRE. Near to the old city of Hebron Mamre was a favourite camping place for Abraham. It had water and shady trees and grass for cattle. Abraham built an altar there, and it was at Mamre that God promised him a son. *Genesis 13. 18.*

MANASSEH. The elder son of Joseph and Asenath born in Egypt. When his ill grandfather, Jacob, was dying he blessed Manasseh with his left hand, and put his right hand on his brother Ephraim's head. In this way the descendants were linked and were associated together in the allotment of land when they came into the Promised Land. *Genesis 48. 8–22.*

MANDRAKE. The mandrake plant is sometimes called the 'love-plant' or the 'love-apple'. It was used as a drug and belongs to the nightshade family. The mandrake perfume was supposed to be a perfume for lovers. *Genesis 30. 14.*

MANGER. 'Laid him in a manger.' So Luke describes what Mary did with her baby son Jesus. The manger was a feeding trough for animals inside a stable. Sometimes it was hollowed out of a rock or stone. *Luke 2. 7.*

MANNA. During their forty years' wanderings from Egypt into the Promised Land under God's guidance the people of Israel used to gather *manna*. Every morning after the dew had gone they found on the ground tiny round balls, or seeds. These tasted sweet and they could be used in baking. The people said, 'What (*man*) is it?', and called it *manna*. The Bible also calls it bread from heaven. In the Sinai desert today little sticky honey balls are found on bushes and drop at night on to the ground. *Exodus 16. 31–35.*

MANOAH. The father of Samson. Before the boy was born an angel appeared to Manoah describing how Samson should be brought up. Both Manoah and his wife saw the vision of the angel and dedicated their son to God. *Judges 13.*

MARANATHA. A phrase in the Aramaic language which means 'Our Lord, Come', or 'Our Lord Cometh'. Paul uses it as a kind of short prayer. *1 Corinthians 16. 22.*

MARK, GOSPEL OF (see also *Gospels*). Mark's book is the second Gospel of the New Testament, but it was the first to be written. It is the shortest and simplest of the Gospels. Many believe that John Mark, the writer of the Gospel, got much of his information from Peter. Seven of his sixteen chapters are about the last few weeks in the life of Jesus. Perhaps Peter remembered these days more vividly than all the rest. John Mark was also a Jerusalem man. He was a friend of Paul and Barnabas as well as Peter. He writes in short, clear sentences as if he was making notes from what he was told by an eye-witness. It is thought that he wrote his Gospel not later than A.D. 70. *Gospel of Mark.*

MARS' HILL (*Areopagus*). A little hill near the Acropolis in Athens where Paul is said to have preached. But it is more likely that Paul spoke to the Council of the Areopagus in the city. The Council originally met on the hill of Ares, Mars or War. *Acts 17. 22.*

MARTHA (see also *Bethany* and *Lazarus*). The sister of Mary and Lazarus of Bethany, one who was always busy in the home, but who was as devoted to Jesus as her sister Mary. The name probably means 'lady' or 'mistress'. It is used only for one person in the Bible. *Luke 10. 38–41.*

MARY. The name Mary in the New Testament is the same as Miriam in the Old Testament. Some say that it means 'beloved'. There are six women of this name in the

Where the animals fed in Bethlehem: stone manger-troughs

New Testament: Mary the mother of Jesus, Mary sister of Martha, Mary Magdalene, Mary the mother of James, Mary the mother of Mark, and Mary 'who worked hard' mentioned by Paul.

Matthew 27. 56; Luke 1. 27; 10. 39; 8. 2; Acts 12. 12; Romans 16. 6.

MASTER. Very often in the Bible the word 'master' is used instead of 'owner' or 'chief'. This happens over a hundred times in the Old Testament. But in the New Testament it means 'teacher' or 'instructor', or is used instead of 'sire' or 'lord'. Jesus is

Was it here that Mary laid her baby?

referred to as 'Master' over twenty times. *2 Kings 5. 1; Mark 10. 17.*

MATTHEW. One of the twelve apostles. Jesus saw him sitting in his office in Capernaum and called him to come and join him. He was a tax-collector and he introduced Jesus to many other tax-collectors and they all had a meal together. Matthew's name appears in all the lists of the twelve apostles. *Matthew 10. 3.*

MATTHEW, GOSPEL OF. The first of the Gospels in the order given in the New Testament. The writer of 'Matthew's Gospel' used what Mark had already written but he adds many other stories about Jesus. He gives the parables of the Tares in the Field, the Unforgiving Debtor, the Ten Virgins. He collects many of the sayings of Jesus together in the 'Sermon on the Mount'. The Gospel of Matthew looks at Jesus through Jewish eyes. It sees him as the long hoped for Messiah of the Jewish people, and also as the King of a Kingdom of God which will include men of all races. *Gospel of Matthew.*

MATTHIAS. One of the first things the little company of Christ's followers did after Jesus had gone away from them into heaven was to choose a new apostle. The place of Judas, who betrayed Jesus, had to be filled. Two names were put forward and after the Jewish custom they drew lots. Matthias was chosen. Very little is known of him. But he must have been close to Jesus. *Acts 1. 23.*

MEAT. The word 'meat' in the Bible usually means 'food' and is best translated that way. *Deuteronomy 2. 6; Matthew 6. 25.*

MEAT OFFERING. In the worship of the Temple the Jews had different kinds of 'offerings' to God. A 'meat-offering' usually referred to a cereal offering in baked cakes of barley or wheat. *1 Chronicles 21. 23.*

MEDES, MEDIA. Media was the ancient name for part of the country we now call Iran, and the Medes were the people who lived in it. They had very stern and unchanging laws. The Books of Daniel and Esther describe the life of the Jews who were captured by the Medes and Persians. *Daniel 6. 8.*

MEGIDDO. The city of Megiddo was one of the strong cities captured by Joshua when he came with his army into the Promised Land. The site of the ancient city lies inland from the port of Haifa. Archaeologists have uncovered at Megiddo the site of the stables for King Solomon's horses. *Joshua 12. 21.*

MELCHIZEDEK. The priest-king of Salem (Jerusalem) who met and blessed Abraham when he came to live in the lands near Jerusalem. When David became king in Jerusalem he claimed to be the successor to Melchizedek. Therefore Jesus, who is of the family of David, is also linked to this most ancient king of Jerusalem. *Hebrews 7. 1–18.*

MELITA. The ancient name for the island of Malta where Paul's ship was driven ashore on his way to Rome. Paul lived for three months on the island and was treated with much kindness. *Acts 28. 1–10.*

MEMPHIS. An Egyptian city on the Nile and one time capital of Egypt. *Hosea 9. 6.*

MENE, MENE, TEKEL AND PARSIN (see also *Belshazzar*). Words probably in Aramaic script which appeared as hand writing on the wall at Belshazzar's feast. It was Daniel who interpreted them as meaning that the king had been weighed in the balances and found wanting. *Daniel 5. 24–28.*

MEPHIBOSHETH. Jonathan's son who was only five years old when his father was killed in battle in 1000 B.C. In the runaway flight his nurse dropped him from her arms and little Mephibosheth was injured and became lame. When David became king he sent for the young man, gave him back all the land belonging to his grandfather

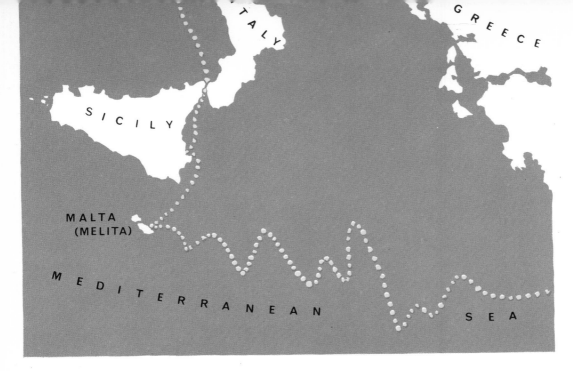

Through the stormy
Mediterranean

and treated him as one of his own sons with a place at his own table. *2 Samuel 9.*

**Paul's ship was blown
ashore on Malta**

MERCY SEAT (see also *Ark of the Covenant*). The most holy thing that the people of

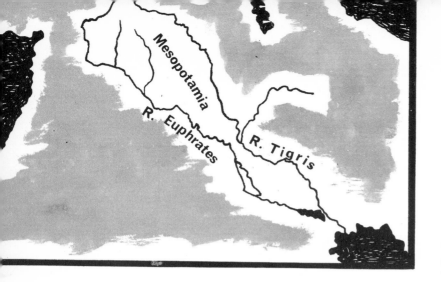

Abraham's country—
between the rivers—Mesopotamia

Israel had was the ark of the covenant. On the top of the ark was a slab of pure gold called the 'mercy-seat' with a cherub at each end. The name in the Hebrew language means *covering*. It was a reminder to the Jews of God's goodness to them. *Exodus 25. 17.*

MEROM, WATERS OF. One of the biggest victories that Joshua and his army won was at the Waters of Merom. Four local kings came out to resist the advance of the Israelites and Joshua beat them all in the battle. Merom lies near the Jordan and not far from the Sea of Galilee. *Joshua 11. 5 ff.*

MESHACH. (*see also Abednego*). One of the three young men in the fiery furnace. But Nebuchadnezzar was astonished to see a fourth, 'like unto the Son of Man'. *Daniel 3. 25.*

MESOPOTAMIA. A word that means 'between the two rivers'—Euphrates and Tigris— which is now partly in Syria and Iraq. This was the land that Abraham came from. It was also the area of the great empires of Assyria and Babylon. Large numbers of Jewish people lived in Mesopotamia. *Genesis 24. 10; Acts 7. 2.*

MESSIAH. The People of Israel always hoped that a great person would one day come among them to set them free from their troubles. It was someone whom God would send, someone who was 'anointed'. 'Messiah' comes from a Hebrew word meaning 'anointed'. The Greek for this word is 'Christos'. It is mentioned only twice in the Old Testament. But this 'hope' that Israel had runs all through the Bible, with many different words attached to it. When Jesus came most Jews did not believe he was the 'Christ' or 'Messiah'. They thought of 'Messiah' as someone quite different from this humble, patient, long-suffering Jesus of Nazareth. But Christians believe that Jesus is the 'Messiah', the one who is the 'hope' of the past and the future too. *Daniel 9. 25; John 1. 41.*

METHUSELAH. The man who is said to have lived for 969 years, the grandfather of Noah. *Genesis 5. 27.*

Secretly they
climbed the
rocky crag of
Michmash—
panic amongst
the Philistines!

MICAH. Micah was one of the active younger prophets living in Judah during the time of Isaiah, about 700 years before Christ. His prophecy is written in the form of a poem. It warns the people of God's anger at many of the things they were doing. He lived in the country near Jerusalem but kept a sharp eye on happenings in the city. He also saw the hard times of the small farmers, and the greed of the big landowners. He pointed out that God wanted justice, humility and mercy in all their life. He also looked for the coming 'Messiah' and foretold that he would be born in Bethlehem. He would bring in the glad and happy time for everyone with peace and goodwill everywhere. *Book of Micah.*

MICHAEL. Perhaps the most famous Michael is the angel in the Book of Revelation who fought the dragon during the war in heaven. *Revelation 12. 7.*

MICHAL. King Saul's younger daughter who was married to David but had no children. *2 Samuel 6. 16–23.*

MICHMASH. In the rocky hills just north of Jerusalem the Philistines and Israelites faced each other at Michmash. One day

Jonathan with his armour-bearer went out on a secret adventure. Climbing up on their hands and feet to the Philistine camp they surprised the enemy. The Philistines thought that hundreds of Israelites were following after Jonathan and got into a panic. It was a gallant escapade which brought a victory to Israel. *1 Samuel 13. 23; 14. 6–15.*

MIDIAN, MIDIANITES. These descendants of Abraham lived in the desert lands of what is now north-west Arabia. They were wanderers, desert dwellers, always ready for a raid. They were expert camel men, and used dromedaries too. Moses had a Midianite wife called Zipporah, and her family helped to guide the people of Israel towards the Promised Land.
Genesis 25. 1–6; Exodus 18.

MILETUS. A one-time important city on the west coast of Asia Minor. But when Paul visited it Miletus was already living on its past glories. *Acts 20. 15.*

MILK. Milk is one of the drinks in the Bible. Cows, goats, sheep and camels all provided milk. It was kept in skin-bottles. To have plenty of milk was a sign of prosperity. It meant that you had many flocks of animals—and that was real wealth.

The Israelites were told that there was plenty of milk as well as honey in Palestine, and that was one of the reasons that encouraged them to get there. *Exodus 3. 8.*

MILL, MILLSTONE. A mill was made up of two large circular stones. They were turned by hand or sometimes by a donkey, and as they turned the grain was crushed into flour. These stones were very heavy indeed. *Matthew 18. 5–6.*

MINISTER, MINISTRY. In the Bible this means one who 'serves' others, or 'serves' God. Jesus called himself a 'minister', and the apostles and their helpers were also called 'ministers'. Paul speaks very proudly of his 'ministry'.
1 Samuel 2. 11; 2 Corinthians 4.

MIRACLES. A miracle in the Bible is God's way of showing his power. Sometimes the word 'miracle' has other words used in its place such as 'wonders', 'signs', 'mighty acts'. But all those words try to describe what happens when a 'miracle' occurs. It is wonderful, mighty and full of meaning. The chief meaning is that God himself is at work. When Jesus was living on earth as God's son he showed God's power by many miracles which the Gospels

106

Milk meant money in early Bible times

Coins were money too— much later

record. The birth, the resurrection and the ascension of Christ are all miracles—showing the wonderful power of God.
Exodus 7. 9; Luke 5. 1–26.

MIRIAM (see also *Mary*). Miriam was a leader amongst the Israelite women in Egypt; and the sister of Moses and Aaron. It was she who knew about the baby Moses being hidden in the bulrushes, and suggested the baby's own mother as his nurse. She sang a song of praise when the Israelites passed over the Red Sea. Her name became a favourite one amongst Jewish families.
Exodus 15. 20.

MITE. The tiniest coin mentioned in the Bible. Made of bronze it was called a *lepton* which means small, or fine. It was worth about $\frac{1}{8}$ cent, or less than a farthing. Jesus noticed a widow putting two of these coins into the collecting box at the Temple. Her gift was the richest of all the gifts—because she put in all she had. *Luke 21. 1–4.*

MITRE. A head-dress worn by the high priest in the Temple worship. It was in the shape of a turban. Fastened on the turban was a plate of gold and on it the words 'Holy to the Lord'. *Exodus 28. 36–39.*

MIZPAH, MIZPEH. These place-names in the Old Testament mean 'watch tower' or 'place for watching'. David took his parents to Mizpeh for safety and Samuel came to Mizpeh to judge the people. It was a place to rally the people on great occasions. An isolated hill about eight miles north of Jerusalem is thought to be Mizpah.
Genesis 31. 44–49; 1 Samuel 7. 16; 22. 3.

MOAB. The high plateau rising to 3000 feet which lies to the east of the Jordan is called Moab. It is cut through by very deep gorges. It was the home of wild people who often raided the land of Israel. *2 Samuel 8. 2.*

MOLECH, MOLOCH. A god in the land of Canaan belonging to the Ammonites. The people of Israel were warned against worshipping this god. Children were sacrificed to him. *Leviticus 18. 21.*

MONEY (see also *Denarius* and *Mite*). It was usual in early Bible times to count a man's wealth in the number of cattle he had. Abraham was rich 'in cattle, silver and gold'. Silver and gold were later used in payments, and these payments were made in rings or ornaments. Then pieces of metal were struck with a seal or design and used for payments. They were called coins. The

'Take up your bed and go home,' said Jesus

107

Jews were careful not to stamp 'images' on their coins. By the time of Jesus, many different coins circulated in Palestine. The

**The first
Moses-basket**

chief coin was the Roman silver coin—the *denarius*. Judas was given thirty of these coins for betraying Jesus—worth a little more than a shilling, or sixteen cents each. *1 Timothy 6. 10.*

MONEY-CHANGERS. In the court of the Temple the money-changers set up their stands. They were there because worshippers brought money gifts to the Temple. If their coins were of the Roman kind they were not accepted in the Temple because they had heathen engravings on them. They had to be in the local coinage minted at Tyre. So there was a lot of changing of money and much trickery in doing so. It was for this that Jesus drove out the money-changers. *Matthew 21. 12–13.*

108

MORDECAI (see also *Haman*). A Jewish exile in Persia where he was employed by King Ahasuerus. He adopted Esther as his daughter. He worked hard against the official adviser Haman who plotted to kill the Jews. His name is greatly honoured in Jewish history. *Esther 3.*

MORIAH. It was to the 'land of Moriah' that Abraham was commanded to take Isaac for sacrifice. Moriah is now thought to be the site of the Temple in Jerusalem itself. *Genesis 22. 2.*

MOSES. Moses was hidden in the bulrushes of the Nile for protection and was found by Pharaoh's daughter. His name means 'one who is drawn out'. He was brought up as an Egyptian in Pharaoh's household with his own mother as nurse. Commissioned and trained by God in the life of the desert, he saw the unhappiness of his people and began to plan to lead them out of Egypt. In the long adventure across the desert to the Promised Land, Moses never failed the people. He got them food and water and was patient when they grumbled. He listened to God speaking to him and on Mount Sinai received the Ten Commandments. His aim was to make the people of Israel into a nation and so train them to be fit to live in the Promised Land: the land he himself never entered. The Jews thought of Moses as their great Leader and Law-Giver. *Book of Exodus.*

MOTE. Why worry about the tiny piece of straw in the eye of your brother, said Jesus, when you have a log of wood in your own? The word *mote* means a dry stalk or twig. Jesus said that if the piece of straw was taken out first then you could see more clearly to help your brother. *Matthew 7. 3–5.*

MULBERRY TREES. The mulberry tree mentioned in the Bible is thought to be a poplar, or aspen tree, or balsam. The Bible story makes the mulberry trees rustle in the wind but it is more likely to be the leaves of a poplar tree.   *2 Samuel 5. 24.*

MULE.   In the Bible lands mules were valuable because they had the strength of a horse and the sure and steady feet of a donkey. Absalom, David's son, was fond

Mulberry tree and evergreen myrtle

of riding his mule. It was on mule-back that he met his death. His hair caught in a branch of a tree but the mule ran on leaving him hanging from the tree and at the mercy of those chasing him.
2 Samuel 18. 9 ff; Psalm 32. 9.

MYRTLE.   A beautiful evergreen plant which sometimes grows as high as thirty feet with scented white flowers. Isaiah speaks of the lovely myrtle replacing the prickly briar. It suggested to him the idea of peace and happiness.   *Isaiah 41. 19.*

The mule was often better than horse or donkey

MYRA.   A port on the south-west tip of Asia Minor in what is now Turkey. It was at Myra that Paul boarded the grain ship on his way to Rome.   *Acts 27. 5–6.*

MYRRH.   One of the gifts the Wise Men gave to the baby Jesus at Bethlehem. It is a sweet-smelling gum found on shrubs in the desert. The gum drips from the shrub on to the ground where it hardens into little round shapes.
Psalm 45. 8; Matthew 2. 11.

N **NAAMAN** (see also *Elisha* and *Gehazi*).
Naaman was the clever general of the king
of Syria but he suffered from the skin
disease of leprosy. In one of his raids he
carried off a little maid to be a servant to
his wife. One day she said to her mistress
that she was sure Elisha, the prophet in
Israel, could cure her master.
So Naaman set off with a
letter to the king of Israel
and a huge present of money
for Elisha. When he came to
Elisha's house, Elisha sent
him a message, 'Go wash in
Jordan seven times.' Naaman
was angry. He said there were
bigger rivers in his own country
to bathe in. But he was
persuaded to dip himself in
Jordan as the prophet
said and he came out cured.
2 Kings 5. 1–14
NABAL (*see Abigail*)
NABOTH. Naboth owned
a vineyard next to the palace
of Ahab, the king of Israel.
The king cast greedy eyes on the
vineyard but Naboth refused to exchange
it for another. It had belonged to his family
for years. But Jezebel, the wicked wife of

'This vineyard is
my family home,' said
Naboth ; 'it is more
precious than money'

Ahab, planned to trick Naboth. She reported that Naboth was heard to swear against the name of God. For this Naboth was stoned to death and the vineyard became the property of Ahab. For this deceitful trickery Ahab and his wife were denounced by Elijah, the prophet.
1 Kings 21. 1–24.

NAHUM. This short prophecy in the Old Testament has only three chapters and was composed more than six hundred years before the time of Jesus. Nahum prophesied the doom of Nineveh. She is bound to be destroyed for her wickedness. The God of Israel, despised by the mighty empire of Assyria, will bring this about for he is the God of all the nations. Nahum is sure that the God of Israel is the controller of the destinies of all peoples and will ultimately be worshipped as the God of all men. *Book of Nahum.*

NAIL. In the Bible a nail might be a finger-nail, a wooden tent peg, or a metal nail or pin. David provided iron nails for the gates of the Temple, but bronze nails were used inside.
1 Chronicles 22. 3; John 20. 25.

NAIN. A few miles from Jesus' own home at Nazareth is the village of Nain. Going there one day he met a funeral procession. A young man had died, the only son of his widow mother. Jesus was very sorry to see the woman crying as she walked along. 'Don't cry' he said to her. Going up to the young man he said, 'I say to you, arise', and to everyone's wonder and fear the young man sat up and began to speak. This is the only mention of Nain in the Bible. *Luke 7. 11–17.*

NAOMI (see also *Boaz* and *Ruth*). A name which means 'my delight'. Naomi's home was in Bethlehem with her husband Elimelech. But they had to leave Bethlehem owing to a famine. They went away to the distant land of Moab with their two sons. There her husband died and so did her two sons. She was left alone with her two daughters-in-law Ruth and Orpah: she decided to go back to Bethlehem. Ruth would not leave her and so Naomi brought her to Bethlehem. There Ruth married Boaz, a kinsman of Naomi's. Their first child, Obed, was—according to custom—considered to be Naomi's too. So Naomi was made very happy in her old age.
Book of Ruth.

Joseph was the carpenter of Nazareth, and probably trained Jesus to the same trade

NAPHTALI. Naphtali was the fifth son of Jacob, and his descendants came into the Promised Land and lived in the area west of the Sea of Galilee. This was an area well known to Jesus. He walked about amongst its villages, and towns such as Bethsaida, Capernaum and Chorazin. It was a smiling land of olives, apricots, figs and vines with plenty of water. *Matthew 4. 12–15.*

NATHAN. There are eleven men of this name in the Old Testament. The best known is the prophet Nathan who lived in the time of King David. God gave him courage to speak to David about his sinful ways. Through Nathan's words God moved David to repentance. *2 Samuel 12. 1–15.*

NATHANAEL. 'Can any good come out of Nazareth?' That was the question that Nathanael asked when Philip told him about Jesus. He did not believe that the great leader they were all looking for could come from such a place. But when Nathanael came to Jesus he found that Jesus knew all about him and his life. He surely must be the King they were expecting. 'Master,' he said, 'you are the Son of God.' *John 1. 43–51.*

NAZARENE. In the early days of Christianity the followers of Jesus of Nazareth were often called Nazarenes. Jesus himself was sometimes called 'Nazarene' to show that he came from Nazareth.
Acts 24. 5.

NAZARETH. The town in Galilee where Jesus lived as a boy with Mary and Joseph. Nazareth was among hills in a high valley and near to the big main roads used by the traders and soldiers. It is likely that the town that Jesus knew was higher up the hills than the present town. Jewish people did not think of Nazareth as an important place. *Luke 2. 39; John 1. 46.*

NAZARITE (see also *Samson*). A 'Nazarite' in the Bible is one who is specially dedicated to the service of God for a certain length of time. He took a vow not to drink wine, or vinegar, or eat raisins. He did not cut his hair. But when the time of the vow was over he cut his hair and burnt it on the altar. Nazarites were not priests but they were regarded as holy men during the time of their vow to God. *Numbers 6. 21.*

NEBO. The mountain range from which Moses viewed the Promised Land which

God did not allow him to enter. It is a mountain that overlooks Jericho.
Deuteronomy 34.

NEBUCHADNEZZAR (see also *Daniel*). The name of the King of Babylon who reigned over that empire six hundred years before Christ. He is often mentioned by the prophets. It was he who captured Jerusalem and took many of the Jews to Babylon. He re-built his capital city of Babylon, and many of the temples in it. He was an able soldier, and also very religious, which made him interested in the religion of the Jews. *2 Kings 24–25.*

NEEDLE'S EYE. It is easier, said Jesus, for a camel to go through a needle's eye than for a rich man to enter the kingdom of God. No camel could do that: it was quite impossible. It was hard for the rich man but with God all things are possible.
Matthew 19. 24–26.

NEGEV. The dry, southern lands of Palestine reaching on towards Egypt are known as the 'Negev' or 'The Dry'. Today they cover over four thousand square miles, or one-half of the area of modern Israel. Mary and Joseph escaped into Egypt with the baby Jesus across this dry land. The Jews tramped across it from Egypt. Today the Jews are working hard to turn it into a cultivated land. *1 Samuel 27. 10.*

NEHEMIAH, BOOK OF. Nehemiah was a Jew who lived in Persia with many other Jews who had been captured by the king of Persia. He worked in the palace of the king and used to get news of what was happening in Jerusalem. One day as Nehemiah served the king with his cup of

The 'hanging' gardens of Babylon built by Nebuchadnezzar to please his wife

wine, the king noticed that Nehemiah's face looked very sad. He told him the reason. He had got news that Jerusalem was an unhappy place — the city walls were down and the gates knocked away and much of the city destroyed. He asked the king's permission to go to Jerusalem to re-build the walls, and the king let him go. When he got to Jerusalem, Nehemiah found that many leading men were against his ideas and tried to stop him. But he rallied the ordinary people and they worked hard to build and to fight off their enemies while they were building under Nehemiah's leadership. The walls of Jerusalem were once again made strong and sound. Nehemiah's book, like that of Ezra, is part of 'history'—the 'history' books of the Bible. Nehemiah lived about 450 years before Jesus came.   *Book of Nehemiah.*

NEIGHBOUR (see also *Samaritans*). 'Who is my neighbour?' That was the question put to Jesus by a lawyer who said he did not know who was his neighbour. Could Jesus tell him? Then Jesus told the parable of the man who was walking along the road from Jerusalem to Jericho. Robbers knocked him down, beat him, took away

his clothes and money and left him half dead. Two very religious men—one of them a priest—were walking along the road and they looked at the poor man but both passed by without helping him. Then came a Samaritan whose nation was usually hated by the Jews. He helped the robbed man, bound up his wounds and took him to the inn and paid the bill. Who was the man's neighbour? asked Jesus. The lawyer knew the answer to the question and so do we. *Luke 10. 29–37.*

NETS. A net is a woven mesh of string used for catching something. The word 'net' is used in different ways in the Bible. Sometimes it means a 'plot' laid by evil men to catch someone off guard. It may mean a net to catch an animal. The disciples of Jesus were fishermen on the Sea of Galilee and used a big drag-net to catch their fish.
Psalm 9. 15;
Isaiah 51. 20;
Luke 5. 4.

NEW MOON. The coming of the new moon was a special time for the people of the Old Testament. The first of each new 'moon', or each month, was a 'holy day.' It was a fresh beginning and the trumpets

'Who is my neighbour?' The Good Samaritan had the answer—and the donkey agreed with him!

were blown. Work was often stopped and there were special services in the Temple. *Isaiah 1. 13ff.*

NEW TESTAMENT (see also *Bible* and *Gospels*). The New Testament is the second part of our Bible and consists of twenty-seven books. First come the Four Gospels; second, the Acts of the Apostles; third, twenty-one letters written by the Apostles and other holy men, and fourthly, the Book of Revelation. All these documents were written during the first hundred years after Jesus lived. They were written by men who had been with Jesus during his life-time, or who knew people who had been with him. These men wrote down what they knew for the churches who were eager to record everything possible about Jesus. The New Testament is the most important book for Christians because it puts together what the first Christians believed about Jesus. It is their testimony to Jesus as the Son of God. It is the story of how Jesus preached the Gospel and of the working of his Spirit in the early church. As the Old Testament shows how all this was prepared for, so the New Testament speaks the final word about God and makes his love to us plain in Jesus Christ.
The New Testament.

NICODEMUS. Nicodemus was an important man amongst the Jews of Jesus' day. He was interested in the teaching of Jesus but was afraid to be seen talking with him. He came secretly by night to Jesus and asked him questions. He wanted to know how he could enter the kingdom of God. 'You must be born again' said Jesus. That answer surprised Nicodemus. Like many other Jews he did not realize that the kingdom which Jesus preached demanded repentance and a new start in life as a follower of Jesus. *John 3. 1–5.*

NICOLAS (or *Nicolaus*). A chosen leader of the church in Antioch. One who became

The River Nile meant food as well as water

a 'deacon' of the church. *Acts 6. 5.*

NILE RIVER. The Bible often speaks of 'the river' meaning the great River Nile. It flows down from Lake Victoria, in the countries of Africa now called Uganda and Tanganyika, for 3000 miles to the Mediterranean Sea. In Bible times, as today, Egypt was very dependent on the Nile to provide water for the crops. Every year the Nile overflowed its banks and spread a rich, muddy soil over the flat lands. Plenty of grain grew in the Nile Valley and people

prophets of the Old Testament spoke of it as a place of wrong-doing. It was the capital of the empire of Assyria far away beyond the great river Euphrates. Its story goes back over four thousand years before Jesus came. It had splendid walls and a fine palace with plenty of water, and over 100,000 people lived in it. About 612 years before Jesus it was conquered by its enemies as the Bible prophets Nahum and Zephaniah said it would be. Ever since then Nineveh has been a heap of rubble. *Nahum 2. 4–10.*

King Og came out to fight, but the Lord said 'Do not fear him'

from far away, like Jacob and his sons, came to get food from Egypt. This made everyone interested in 'the river' and the people who lived along its banks.
Exodus 2. 5; Isaiah 23. 10.

NIMROD. Genesis (*Ch.* 10) says that Nimrod was a mighty hunter. There are many legends and stories about him which do not appear in the Bible. He was a grandson of Ham the son of Noah, and the land where he lived was Assyria far to the north of Palestine of which the city of Nineveh was the capital. It was sometimes called the 'Land of Nimrod'. *Micah 5. 6.*

NINEVEH (see also *Jonah*). Nineveh is one of the 'wicked' cities of the Bible. The

NOAH (see also *Ark* and *Flood*). Noah, to the men of the Bible, is one of the great fathers of the human race. He was told by God that the Flood would come so he had ample time to build the Ark and arrange for the safety of his family and the animals. Noah was a good man and to him God made a promise, a 'covenant' that never again would he destroy men and the living creatures of the world. We are reminded of the promise when we see the rainbow in the sky. Noah had three sons, Shem, Ham and Japheth, whose descendants are scattered all over the world. It is most likely he had many other children too.
Genesis 6-8; Hebrews 11. 7.

NUMBERS, BOOK OF. This is the fourth book in the Bible. It takes its name from the count of the people which Moses—under God's command—ordered when they were in the desert of Sinai. The book gives the 'numbers' of the various tribes with exact lists of the various families. Then it gives very careful instructions about the ways in which the Israelites are to behave both in their families and in worship. It is a 'Law' book and is part of the 'law of Moses', which the Jews obeyed. Moses is

OBED (see also *Boaz*, *Ruth* and *Naomi*). The son of Ruth and Boaz and the grandfather of David. The birth of the little boy brought much happiness to Naomi who thought of him as her own child and nursed him affectionately. *Ruth 4. 17.*

OBEY, OBEDIENCE. These words come very often in the Bible. The word really means 'hearken to' or 'listen to' or 'to give heed to'. This is what God was always trying to get the Israelites to do—to listen to him, to obey and to love him. In the

The olive tree— symbol of beauty and strength, of peace and friend- ship—p.118

the great man of the book and he speaks of the holy God who is to be worshipped and obeyed. Very detailed instructions are given in the Book of Numbers which shows how God entered into every part of the life of the people of Israel. *Book of Numbers.*

OBADIAH. The short poem-prophecy of the prophet Obadiah comes towards the end of the Old Testament and may have been spoken and written about 600 years before Christ. The shortest Old Testament book, it describes the misery that came to Jerusalem when it was captured by the Babylonians. It also speaks out against the Edomites (descendants of Esau). *Book of Obadiah.*

New Testament Jesus showed that obedience to God is part of men's love to God and that God has a fatherly love towards them. *1 Samuel 15. 22; Philippians 2. 8ff.*

OG. King Og of Bashan was a mighty warrior and king of over sixty cities in the Promised Land. All the cities had high walls, and big gates. Og was huge in size and was said to sleep on a vast iron bedstead specially made for him. The Israelite army defeated him in the battle of Edrei and the news of Og's downfall terrified the land and made Israel's advance much easier. *Deuteronomy 3. 1–11.*

OIL (see also *Olive Trees*). Oil was used in Bible times in many different ways. It came chiefly from the berries on the olive trees which grew almost everywhere in Palestine. Oil was used in cooking, in lighting the lamps, in the worship of the Temple. It was used as a medicine and on the face and body to make the skin soft and smooth. A supply of oil was one of the most important things to have in any Jewish home. *2 Kings 4. 2ff; Matthew 25. 1–13.*

OINTMENT (see also *Anointing*). As Jesus sat in the house of Simon the leper in Bethany, a woman came with a jar of ointment and poured it on his head as he sat at the table. The ointment was perhaps a jar of beautifully scented olive oil. In Bible times people often used ointment of this kind on the head and body. *Matthew 26. 6–13.*

OLD TESTAMENT (see also *Bible*). The Old Testament is the first part of the Bible. It was the Bible that Jesus knew and is divided into three main sections—the Law, the Prophets, the Writings. The Law books are the first five books of the Bible called 'the book of Moses'; the Prophets include Joshua, Judges, Samuel, Kings, Isaiah, Jeremiah and Ezekiel and the shorter books of the prophets at the end of the Old Testament; the Writings are the rest of the Old Testament such as Psalms, Proverbs, Daniel and Chronicles. The total is thirty-nine books. In the Old Testament we read of the works, wonders and words of God. It shows how God made himself known to the people of Israel. They became 'his' people and he was 'their' God. It shows how the people often forgot about God, and were disobedient to his law and his ways. It describes how they were prepared for the coming of God's Son, Jesus Christ. The early Christians used the Old Testament to show that the Messiah it speaks of had come in Jesus Christ. It was their Bible and is ours too. *The Old Testament.*

OLIVE, OLIVE TREES. The olive berry grew on the olive tree which reached as high as twenty feet. The trunk of the olive tree was twisted and it had many branches which gave a shady place to sit when the sun was hot. The olive berries ripened in the early autumn. Sometimes the trees were beaten with sticks and the berries fell off on to the ground in heaps. The berries were crushed in the olive press and the oil that came out was stored in jars. The olive berry was also pickled and eaten with bread. The wood of the olive tree was used as firewood, and in all sorts of ways the olive tree was a friend to the people of the Bible. *Judges 9. 8ff; Romans 11. 17ff.*

OLIVES, MOUNT OF. A group of hills that overlooks Jerusalem across the Kidron Valley, and offers a fine view of the city. The highest point reaches 2723 feet. The Mount of Olives (or Olivet) that Jesus knew, unlike today, was thickly wooded with many olive trees. Jesus undoubtedly walked over these hills for this is the area of the Garden of Gethsemane and also the reputed mount of the Ascension. *Matthew 24. 3; Acts 1. 12.*

OMRI. Omri was a king of Israel about nine hundred years before Christ. He was chosen by the army to be king, and he reigned for twelve years. *1 Kings 16. 16.*

ONESIMUS (see also *Philemon*). The letter of Paul which he wrote to his friend Philemon is all about Onesimus. Onesimus was

a 'slave' and he legally belonged to Philemon. He had been with Paul and had become a Christian. Now Paul sends him back to Philemon and asks him to treat him not like a 'slave' but as a 'brother'. The name 'Onesimus' means 'useful'—a name very often given to 'slaves'.
Epistle to Philemon.

ONESIPHORUS. In writing his letters, Paul always remembered to send kind messages to his friends who had helped him. One of them was Onesiphorus whose home was in Ephesus. He never forgot Paul and came to see him when he was in prison in Rome. Onesiphorus cheered him

Over the seas to Ophir and its gold. But where was Ophir?

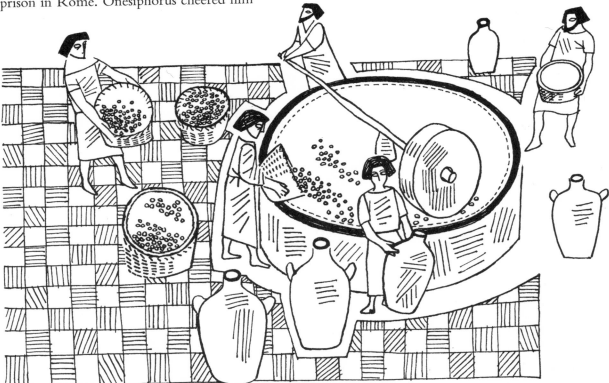

Olive oil— crushed by the millstone and stored in jars

up and was true to his name which means 'profit-bringer'. *2 Timothy 1. 16ff.*

OPHIR. The land of Ophir to the men of the Old Testament was the land where gold came from. Solomon sent his ships down the Red Sea to Ophir. But no one is quite sure where Ophir is. Was it in the land of Arabia or somewhere along the east coast of Africa, or right across the Indian Ocean near Bombay? *1 Kings 9. 28.*

119

ORACLE. In the Bible, this word stands for the 'words' or the 'teaching' of God. It refers to God's 'promises' and God's 'truth'. The 'oracles' of God are to be respected and honoured for they come from God himself. *Psalm 28. 2; Acts 7. 38.*

OREB. Oreb was one of the princes of Midian killed in the fighting against Gideon and his gallant men. *Judges 7. 25.*

ORGAN. The word comes four times in King James Old Testament. It does not mean the kind of organ we know. It was a pipe, or a group of pipes, blown in the mouth. *Job 21. 12; Psalm 150. 4.*

ORPAH (see also *Naomi*). Orpah was one of Naomi's daughters-in-law who lived in the land of Moab. The other was Ruth. When her husband died Orpah took Naomi's advice and went home again to her own family. *Ruth 1. 15.*

ORPHAN. The Old Testament gave very careful instructions to the Jews about their duty to children who had no fathers. The word 'fatherless', which is sometimes used, gives the meaning of the word exactly. The 'orphan' child had a rightful share in everything. The Bible says that God cares for the 'fatherless' and watches over them. *Deuteronomy 24. 17; Lamentations 5. 3.*

OSTRICH. 'The wings of the ostrich wave proudly'; so writes the author of Job. Then he describes how the ostrich lays her eggs and leaves them in the earth where they can easily get crushed. She is cruel to her young, but when she runs, her long legs give her greater speed than the horse. There is no mention of the ostrich in the New Testament. *Job 39. 13–18.*

The pipe and the harp (both big and little) make music in the Bible

OVEN (see also *Bread*).   The oven for baking bread was a large round earthen jar. It was heated by a fire inside. When the sides of the jar were really hot the flat cakes of dough were spread on the sides, and were gradually baked through.
Psalm 21. 9; Matthew 6. 30.

PALESTINA, PALESTINE.   The name of the land which God promised to the Israelites when they left Egypt. Today the land of 'Palestine' is divided into two countries—Israel and Jordan. The land is also known as 'Philistia', 'Canaan', 'The Promised Land' or 'The Holy Land'.
Exodus 15. 14ff; Deuteronomy 19. 8.

PALM.   The palm tree is often mentioned in the Bible. It is a tall, slender tree without branches. At the top of the palm tree is a tuft of leaves which grow very long. The Bible palm tree grew dates amongst its leaves. The tree gave food to eat, wood from its long trunk, rope and matting from its leaves, wine from its sap and seeds for camels' food. It was a very valuable tree.
Psalm 92. 12; John 12. 13.

PALSY.   'My servant lieth at home sick of the palsy.' So said the Roman centurion to Jesus. 'Only speak the word,' he said, 'and my paralysed servant will be healed. I am not worthy for you to come into my house.' Jesus marvelled at the man's faith and then cured the servant. Palsy is a Bible word for paralysis.   *Matthew 8. 6.*

PAMPHYLIA.   A district that runs along the coast of south Asia Minor which Paul visited on his first journey. One of its chief cities was Perga with a famous temple.
Acts 13. 13.

PAPER, PAPYRUS.   In Bible times 'paper' came from the papyrus plant which grew in rivers, lakes and marshes. From the inside of its stalks came a pith. This was cut into strips and then laid side by side and beaten together. This made a smooth white sheet of 'paper' which could be written on,

both sides. Parts of the Old Testament and the New Testament were written on papyrus rolls. Mark's Gospel needed a roll of papyrus 19 feet long. But as more and more copies were needed flat sheets of papyrus were used, arranged in book form.
2 John 12.

PAPHOS.   On the island of Cyprus—a town visited by Paul where he met the false prophet, Bar-Jesus.   *Acts 13. 6.*

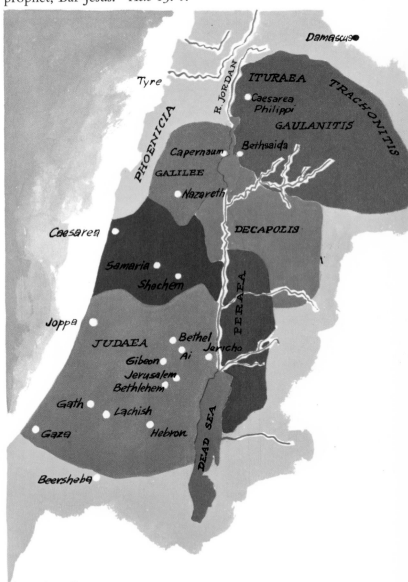

Palestine—the Promised Land between sea and desert—in the days of Jesus

PARABLES. Jesus often told a 'parable' to his listeners to help them understand the real meaning of what he was saying. It meant 'saying things in a different way', or 'putting things side by side in story form.' He told 'parables' about events such as the sower sowing his seed, the seed growing secretly, the mustard seed, the lost sheep and the lost coin and the foolish virgins. Sometimes Jesus explains the meaning of the parable but often he expects his hearers to work it out for themselves. The parables of Jesus have an inner meaning which becomes clear as you think about them. *Psalm 78. 2; Matthew 13. 18; Mark 4. 33.*

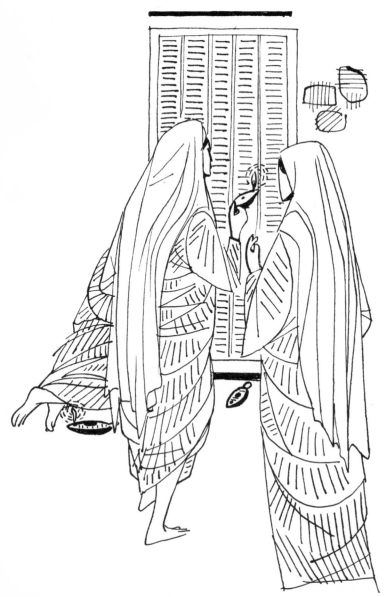

The lamps are going out! (Parable of the Foolish Virgins)

PARADISE. 'Paradise' was thought of as a 'garden', a 'pleasant' place, a 'glorious' world to be in. The Jews also thought of 'paradise' as a wonderful time in the future when all their messianic hopes would come true. The last chapters of Revelation describe paradise as a 'garden of God' in which the beauty and glory of God's plans for a 'new heaven and a new earth' are fully realized. *Revelation 21–22.*

PARAN. A part of the wilderness of the Sinai desert where Hagar and Ishmael were sent to live. *Genesis 21. 21.*

PARCHMENT (see also *Paper*). Parchment was made from the skins of goats and sheep. Parts of the Bible were written on it. It was not so often used as papyrus but it lasted longer. *2 Timothy 4. 13.*

PARTHIANS. Parthia is an area to the south-east of the Caspian Sea. Many Jews captured by the kings of Persia lived there. It may have been some of these Jews, called Parthians, who were visiting Jerusalem on the day of Pentecost. *Acts 2. 9.*

PASHHUR. Pashhur was one of the young men in the court of King Zedekiah who plotted against the prophet Jeremiah. He threw Jeremiah into the slimy pit from where he was rescued by Ebedmelech. *Jeremiah 38. 1–6.*

PASSION. The Bible twice mentions this word as meaning 'desires'. But Christ's 'passion' means his suffering and death for our sake. *Acts 1. 3; 14. 15; James 5. 17.*

PASSOVER. This is the great Jewish feast which reminds the Jews of God's goodness to them in the land of Egypt. When disaster came to Egypt every Israelite house that had blood sprinkled on the doorpost was 'passed over' and saved from destruction. The 'pass over' became a feast of remembrance when the 'pass over' lamb was killed. Jesus and his disciples ate their 'passover' together as a family meal.

Christians celebrate this 'Last Supper' as 'The Lord's Supper', or 'Holy Communion'. *Exodus 12; Luke 22.*

PATMOS. A Greek island off the coast of Turkey to which the apostle John was banished in A.D. 95. The island is eight miles long and four miles wide with high and rugged hills. Some of the wonderful descriptions given in the Book of Revelation are said to come from the wild scenery of Patmos. *Revelation 1. 9.*

PAUL. Paul is the greatest apostle in the New Testament. He was said to be a small man with crooked legs and with poor eyesight. He was born in the town of Tarsus, now in modern Turkey, and then part of the Roman Empire. His parents were Jews and they called him Saul. But he was also a Roman citizen, and had a good education. He lived during the days of Jesus but we do not know whether he

Frequently on the move—the Patriarchs carried their wealth with them

PATRIARCH. The name means 'head of the family'. The three great patriarchs of the Israelites are Abraham, Isaac and Jacob, who lived nearly two thousand years before Jesus came. They were the 'fathers' of all the 'people'. They moved about with their families and their cattle sometimes settling in one place but always ready to move to new pastures for their flocks. The Israelites looked back on the days of the patriarchs as wonderful times. It was the patriarchs to whom the one true God was first revealed. *Acts 7. 8.*

ever saw Jesus. He grew up to hate the teachings of Jesus and worked hard to stop their spreading. Then he was converted to the Christian way in a wonderful manner on the road to Damascus and began to preach about Jesus. The Jews hated him for this and did their best to stop him. The Christians too at first were not very friendly. Paul went home to Tarsus and preached about Jesus there. Then he began to travel further afield along the coast of Asia Minor. He preached chiefly to those who were non-Jews. He crossed over the sea to Greece and preached in the famous cities of Salonika, Athens and Corinth. He wrote letters to many of the churches, some of which are in the New Testament. In these letters he says what the love of Jesus Christ meant to him and what a difference it had made in his life. His letters show him to be a man of warm heart and tender affection but above all a man whose love towards Christ filled all his life. His last journey was to Rome where it is believed he was put to death by the Emperor Nero in A.D. 67. *Galatians 1. 11–24; 2. 1–10.*

PEACOCKS. When King Solomon's ships brought home gold and silver they also brought some peacocks. Whether Solomon's peacocks were like the lovely, brightly plumed birds that we know is not made clear in the story. The peacock's true home is in India and Ceylon but the peacock was also known in Athens nearly five hundred years before the days of Jesus. *1 Kings 10. 22.*

PEARLS. 'Finding one pearl of great value, he sold all that he had and bought it.' That is how Jesus described the merchant who bought and sold pearls. The kingdom of God was like the beautiful pearl. It is worth giving up everything to have it. Pearls found in shellfish were highly valued in Bible times and worth a lot of money. *Matthew 13. 45.*

PENIEL. When Jacob went out to meet his brother Esau he crossed the Jabbok brook and gave the spot the name Peniel, which means 'the face of God'. *Genesis 32. 30–31.*

PENTATEUCH (see also *Old Testament*). The first five books of the Old Testament are called the *Pentateuch*. It comes from a Greek word meaning 'five-books'. The five books are Genesis, Exodus, Leviticus, Numbers and Deuteronomy. They describe how God created the world, how he dealt with Noah, Abraham and Moses and other famous men in the history of the Israelites. The books also describe how the people came out of Egypt into the Promised Land, how they received God's law and became his own people. The books tell the wonderful story of God's goodness to the people of Israel and show how through all the years of their life God trained and taught the people to worship and obey him. *Genesis, Exodus, Leviticus, Numbers, Deuteronomy.*

PENTECOST (see also *Feasts*). This is a Jewish feast, and the word means 'fifty'. Pentecost came fifty days after the Passover. It marked the end of the barley harvest when the Jewish people presented freshly baked loaves of fine new flour to the Temple. It was on the day of Pentecost that the disciples of Jesus were gathered in Jerusalem and the Holy Spirit came upon them like a powerful wind. That day of Pentecost marked the beginning of the Christian Church. *Acts 2. 1–4.*

PEOR. The name of a god worshipped by some of the Israelites on their way into the Promised Land. This local god belonged to the Moabite people and many Israelites went to the sacrifices. God ordered Moses to punish all those who had worshipped Peor—a lesson the Israelites did not quickly forget. *Numbers 25. 3.*

PERDITION. A word used in the New Testament to mean 'destruction', or 'perish-ing'. Judas Iscariot is called 'son of Perdition'. *John 17. 12.*

PERGA.—see *Pamphylia.*

PERGAMUM. One of the 'seven churches of Asia' listed in the Book of Revelation. Pergamum, or Pergamos, was an important city and centre of the Roman rule and reported to be an evil city. *Revelation 1. 11.*

PERSIA, PERSIANS (see also *Nehemiah*). Five hundred years before Christ the Persians ruled a strong and important empire to the north and east of Palestine. The prophets in the Old Testament speak about them and warn the people of how God will use the Persians to punish them. When the

Persia—a land of skilled artists and horsemen

Persians conquered the city of Babylon they gave permission to the Jews to take back the precious vessels of the Temple to Jerusalem and to re-build the walls of the city. The Persians were educated, skilful people who built great palaces and decorated them beautifully. They worshipped many different kinds of gods. It may be that the Wise Men who came to visit the baby Jesus in Bethlehem were from Persia. *The Book of Ezra.*

PETER. Peter always stands first in the list of the disciples of Jesus. He was one of those who were very close to Jesus. As a working fisherman he was called 'Simon' but Jesus gave him the name 'Peter' which means 'rock' or 'stone'. It was Peter who boldly said that Jesus was the Christ, the Son of God, and it was Peter who later denied that he knew Jesus. Peter was the leader of the apostles and although he was a Jew he came to see that Christ's gospel was for all men. Peter went to Rome and it is believed that he was put to death there for his faith in Christ during the reign of the Emperor Nero. *Matthew 16. 13–23.*

PETER, EPISTLES OF. There are two short letters in the New Testament called the first and second letters of Peter. The letters are different in their style of writing, but they both speak to Christians in the churches of Asia Minor about faith in Jesus Christ. They call on Christians to have love towards one another, to put away evil things from their lives and to remember what Jesus would have them do. The two letters are really 'sermons' such as Peter would have preached to the churches he wrote to. It may be that Peter wrote his letters from Rome during the time of persecution under the Emperor Nero. *Epistles of Peter.*

PHARAOH. This is the name the Bible uses for the kings of Egypt. It is like saying 'His Majesty'. It means 'great house'. There are many different Pharaohs mentioned in the Bible. The one who is mentioned most is the Pharaoh who oppressed the people of Israel in Egypt. He was called Rameses II. *Exodus 9. 1–7.*

As the cock crew Peter denied Christ

PHARISEES. In the days of Jesus Christ the Pharisees were a group of Jews dedicated to keeping the Jewish law in every exact detail. The name means 'the separate ones'. They numbered about 6000 and they believed that the Jewish law had 600 commandments which it was their duty to keep and to see that other people did so too. They were especially anxious to see that 'one-tenth' (tithe) of everything was given to the Temple and to God's worship. They believed that all the unhappy events in the history of the Jews had come about because the people did not keep God's law. Jesus was angry with them because they could not see beyond the very little points of the law to the larger law of love towards all men. They were good men who thought that obedience to every little bit of the Jewish law was necessary to be truly God's servants. Jesus showed a new and better way which the Pharisees failed to understand. *Matthew 5. 20; Acts 26. 4ff.*

PHILADELPHIA. One of the 'seven churches of Asia' mentioned in the Book of Revelation. It was in the Roman province of Asia, and was famous for its temples and religious festivals. The word is a Greek one meaning 'brotherly love'. *Revelation 3. 7.*

PHILEMON, EPISTLE TO (see also *Onesimus*). This is a very short letter of Paul to his friend Philemon in Colossae and is all about a slave called Onesimus who by law belonged to his master Philemon. Onesimus was kind and helpful to Paul, and in the letter Paul asks Philemon to take Onesimus back and be kind to him in return. Paul says that Onesimus comes back to Philemon not as a returned slave but as a Christian brother who is loved both by Paul and Philemon. *Epistle to Philemon.*

PHILIP. Philip 'the apostle' was called to follow Jesus on the day after Andrew and Peter. He too may have been a fisherman as he lived at Bethsaida on the Sea of Galilee. He was with Jesus at the feeding of the Five Thousand. Philip 'the evangelist' was an active missionary of the early church. It was he who converted the ambassador of the Queen of Ethiopia on the desert road at Gaza. He was one of the first seven 'deacons' chosen by the church. *John 1. 43–46; Acts 8. 26–40.*

Rameses II— Pharaoh of Egypt who oppressed the Israelites, and treated them as slaves

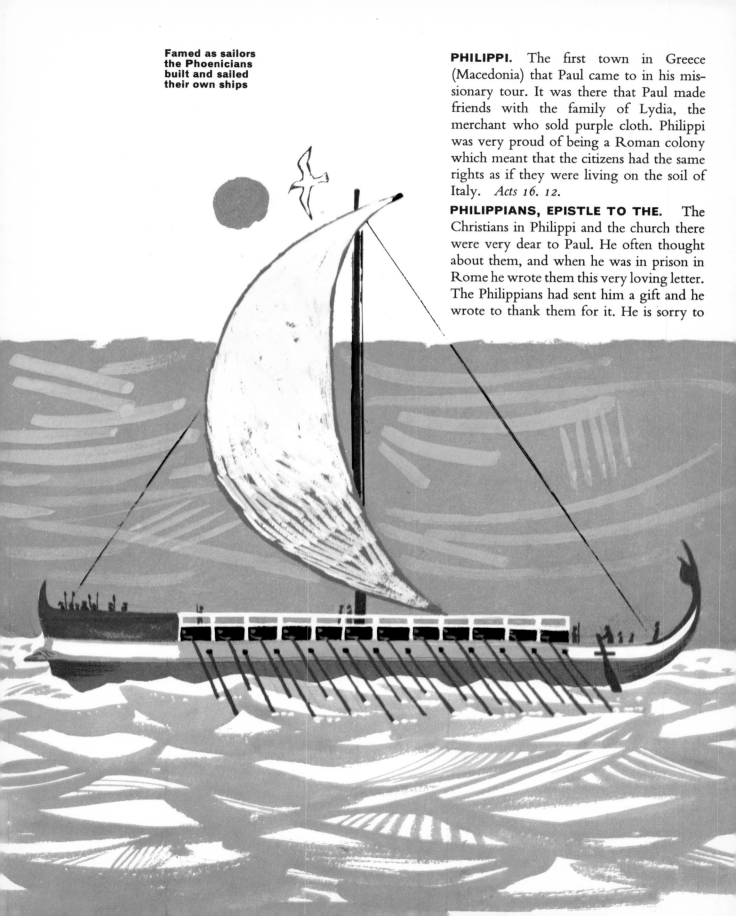

Famed as sailors the Phoenicians built and sailed their own ships

PHILIPPI. The first town in Greece (Macedonia) that Paul came to in his missionary tour. It was there that Paul made friends with the family of Lydia, the merchant who sold purple cloth. Philippi was very proud of being a Roman colony which meant that the citizens had the same rights as if they were living on the soil of Italy. *Acts 16. 12.*

PHILIPPIANS, EPISTLE TO THE. The Christians in Philippi and the church there were very dear to Paul. He often thought about them, and when he was in prison in Rome he wrote them this very loving letter. The Philippians had sent him a gift and he wrote to thank them for it. He is sorry to hear of troubles in the church and he warns them against evil things. Paul writes very tenderly about himself and his faith in Jesus. Although he is a Jew he is proud to be a Christian, a humble follower of Jesus, and he presses on toward 'the goal for the prize of the upward call of God in Christ Jesus.' He asks the Philippians to think about the lovely, true and just things in life and to make their manner of living worthy of the Gospel. This letter is one of Paul's finest and shows his loving care of the Philippians. *Epistle to the Philippians.*

PHILISTINES. The strip of land along the southern part of Palestine was called Philistia and there the Philistines lived. From the sea coast the Philistines were always pressing inland to the hills of Judah and making raids on the lands of the Israelites. Saul and David fought regularly against the Philistines, a fierce, warlike people. They had their own gods—Dagon, Ashtoreth and Baalzebub, and their five main cities were Gaza, Ashkelon, Ashdod, Ekron and Gath. They involved the Israelites in much warfare until King David finally put an end to their power. *2 Samuel 5. 17ff.*

PHINEHAS. A grandson of Aaron and therefore a priest by descent. He was a priest to the people in the time of the Judges. Another Phinehas, a son of the old priest Eli, was killed in battle with the Philistines guarding the Ark of God. *Exodus 6. 25; 1 Samuel 4.*

PHOEBE. Phoebe was a generous woman of the church at Cenchreae near Corinth. The name means 'radiant'. She was a 'deaconess' of the church and helped many travellers who passed through the port of Corinth. Paul was grateful to her for her kindness. *Romans 16. 1–2.*

PHOENICIA. The land of 'Tyre and Sidon' which the Bible refers to is the ancient land of Phoenicia that runs along the eastern Mediterranean–Levant coast. It is now the land of Lebanon. Its people were famous sailors and had ships sailing the seas bringing home cargoes of timber, gold, and silver. When they were persecuted in Jerusalem some of the first Christians went over the border to live in Phoenicia. Paul landed at Tyre on his way to Jerusalem. *1 Kings 5; Acts 11. 19.*

PHRYGIA. A large area of land in what is now modern Turkey. Many Jews lived there and they are mentioned in the list of people present in Jerusalem on the day of Pentecost. Paul travelled and preached in Phrygia. *Acts 16. 6.*

PHYLACTERY.—see *Frontlets.*

PILATE. Pontius Pilate was Roman governor of Judaea during the time of Jesus. He had full control of the land, and was general of the Roman army. He appointed the high priests and had charge of the Temple and its money which annoyed the Jews very much. He had the power to condemn a man to death and for that reason Jesus was brought before him. He was a weak man in character, and by sending Jesus to be crucified he was pleasing the Jewish leaders, perhaps against his own conscience. *Mark 15.*

'What evil has he done?' asked Pilate

PINE. The pine tree or the fir tree are evergreen trees which grow on the hills of Palestine. Pinewood is good for building and Solomon used it in his temple. Isaiah speaks of the growing pine tree as a sign that even trees would flourish in the desert. *Isaiah 41. 19.*

PIPE. A musical instrument made of reed, and played by blowing through a hole. The pipers played in processions of rejoicing and also at funerals. The note on a pipe was like the sound of a whistle. Children loved to play 'pipers' in the streets. *Matthew 11. 17.*

PITCHER. An earthenware jar for carrying or storing water. *Luke 22. 10.*

PLAGUE. The Bible often uses the word *plague* to mean something 'very bad' like a disease or an illness afflicting everybody. It comes from a word that means 'to beat' or 'to smite'. When the Israelites were in Egypt God sent ten plagues to 'smite' the Egyptians—the fish in the Nile all died; there was a swarm of frogs; a swarm of mosquitoes; a plague of flies; a plague of boils; heavy hail; locusts; a dust storm; cattle died; first born babies died. Sometimes it was famine, or disease. *Exodus 7–11.*

PLOUGH. The plough in the Bible was usually wooden with one handle. It was made of oak, and had a sharp nose. It was pulled by an ox and made a furrow through the stony soil. The ploughman had to keep his eye always on the ox and on the plough. He had to guide the plough and the ox. He could not look back and do his job well. When Jesus said that no one putting his hand to the plough and looking back is fit for the kingdom of God he meant that no one could be a good disciple if he kept longing for his old way of life.
Luke 9. 62.

PLUMBLINE, PLUMMET. A plumbline was a piece of cord weighted with lead (the plummet). It was used to check the work of the builder to see whether his walls were upright. The prophet Amos said that God measured Israel in the same way. *Isaiah 28. 17; Amos 7. 7–9.*

The plough drove through the stony soil—but it needed a sharp nosed ploughshare of wood, or iron

POETRY (see also *Psalms*).   There is much poetry in the Bible, for the Hebrew people were fond of songs and poems. The biggest collection of poetry is in the Psalms. Many of the prophets also spoke, or wrote, their prophecies in the form of poems. Hebrew poetry has rhythm but not rhyme. It has many wonderful pictures of the sky, the sea, the mountains, the land and its beauty —all of which speak about God and his goodness.   *The Psalms; The Prophets.*

PONTUS.   A big area of what is today Turkey bordering on the Black Sea. Jews from Pontus were at Jerusalem on the day of Pentecost.   *Acts 2. 9.*

POOL.   A pool of water was always a wonderful sight to see in dry and thirsty lands such as the Bible writes about. But there were also 'pools' inside the cities fed through tunnels connected with a spring of water outside the city walls, such as the Pool of Siloam.   *Isaiah 35. 7; John 9. 7.*

POTIPHAR.   When the Midianites brought Joseph into Egypt they sold him as a slave to Potiphar, a high official of Pharaoh. It was in Potiphar's household that Joseph grew up and became the chief steward. *Genesis 37. 36.*

As the wheel turned so the pot grew

POTSHERD.   A piece of broken earthenware. When they are digging in Bible lands archaeologists always look out for potsherds. It helps them to identify the people who lived on the spot and when they lived there.   *Job 2. 8; Psalm 22. 15.*

POTTAGE.   A tasty soup made of red lentils, a very common dish in the days of Abraham, Isaac and Jacob. It was for a dish of pottage that Esau traded his birthright to Jacob.   *Genesis 25. 29-34.*

POTTER, POTTERY.   'Arise, go down to the potter's house.' That was God's com-

No plough without a share

mand to Jeremiah. There he saw the potter take the clay in his hands, press it together, split it up, and throw some pieces away. He watched him turn his wheel and noticed that one pot broke off and the potter had to begin all over again. That is how God deals with people and with nations, said Jeremiah. God is like a potter making and re-making all the time. Every village in Bible times had its potter who made the pots used in the homes of the people. *Jeremiah 18. 1–6.*

PRAETORIUM (or *Judgment Hall*). The name given to the headquarters of a Roman army. When Pilate handed Jesus over to the soldiers they took him inside the praetorium and began to mock him. Paul too was guarded by soldiers in a praetorium. The name was also used for the residence of a Roman governor, where he gave judgment. *Matthew 27. 27; Acts 23. 35.*

PRIEST (see also *Aaron*). Priests in the Bible are descended from Aaron, the first high priest. Their first and supreme duty was to guard the Ark of God. They also had to teach the people how to keep the law of Moses and to watch over the ways in which they did it. In the Temple it was the priest who conducted the worship. *Exodus 28. 1; Joshua 3.*

PRISON. Prisons are frequently mentioned in the Bible. They were dark, windowless dungeons below the ground, and prisoners were bound by chains. Some famous men in the Bible, Joseph, Jeremiah, Samson, John the Baptist, Peter and Paul suffered in prisons for the sake of their faith. Paul even converted the jailer who was guarding him! *Genesis 39. 20; Mark 6. 17; Acts 16. 19–34.*

PROCONSUL. The Roman Empire was organized into provinces and the governor of each province was called a 'proconsul', which means a 'deputy'. *Acts 18. 12.*

PROPHET (see also *Old Testament*). A prophet in the Bible is a man who speaks in the name of God. There are several types of prophets. Abraham was the 'first' prophet and Moses is the 'great' prophet. It is God who 'makes' the prophet and gives him his message and the truth that he is to preach. The prophet speaks about the happenings of life as he sees them and shows how God is using these events to teach his truth. The prophet is not afraid to speak to kings and governors as well as ordinary people. He sees God at work everywhere and in all things. Sometimes the prophet speaks in story or parable form, to make his message clear. In the Old Testament the books of the prophets are in two sections—the 'former' prophets, such as Samuel and Elijah, and the 'later' prophets which include Isaiah and Jeremiah. Then at the end of the Old Testament there are 'twelve' prophets' from Hosea to Malachi often called the 'minor' prophets. *The Prophets.*

PROSELYTE. Anyone who was converted to the Jewish faith was called a 'proselyte'. The word means 'a stranger'—someone who comes in from the outside. *Acts 2. 10.*

PROVERBS, BOOK OF. The Book of Proverbs belongs to the books of the Bible called the 'wisdom' books. It brings together wise sayings about how to live a good, happy and religious life. Many of the Proverbs are thought to be those of the wise King Solomon. These hundreds of proverbs were gathered together over many years and may have been put into one book about four hundred years before Jesus came. Jesus knew the book as part of his Bible and the New Testament has many quotations from it. *Book of Proverbs.*

PSALMS, BOOK OF (see also *Poetry*). For many people the Book of Psalms is the most loved book in the Old Testament. It is poetry and hymns put together. Its poems are meant to be sung, for the Jewish people sang the Psalms in their Temple worship. They called it the 'songs of praise' book. All the experiences of human life are found in the Psalms—sorrow, gladness, sin, suffering, goodness, evil. This has made the Psalms a much read and used book. The name of David is given to over seventy of the Psalms. The Psalms was the prayer-book that Jesus used and he often quoted from it. In the Psalms he found himself very close to God his Father as millions of other people do when they read or sing the Psalms. It brings together so much of the teaching of the Bible about God and man that it has been called a 'Bible within the Bible'. *Book of Psalms*.

PUBLICAN. The New Testament uses this word to mean a man who collected taxes on behalf of the Romans. He often tried to get more than he was entitled to and this gave him a bad name and made him hated by the people. The Jews in

'Have you not known' said Isaiah the Prophet 'the Lord is the Creator of the ends of the earth'

133

particular hated the 'publicans' because they mixed with the Gentiles and even had meals with them and therefore were thought to be unclean. *Matthew 9. 10–12.*

PURIFICATION.   All through the early books of the Old Testament runs the idea that the people of Israel were to be a 'holy' people. They were to keep themselves 'clean' and exact instructions are given in the Book of Leviticus about this. They were told exactly what they could eat, how they could dress and how to behave. If by a mistake they ate something or did something which was unclean there had to be a ceremony of purification. Usually this meant bathing the body in water and washing the clothes.
Leviticus 15. 7; Numbers 31. 23; Luke 2. 22.

PURIM.   The annual festival of the Jewish people to give God thanks for their preservation in Persia. *Esther 9. 26.*

Q QUAIL.   As they travelled across the Sinai wilderness to the Promised Land God provided food for the people of Israel. The wind blowing in from the sea used to bring flocks of small birds called quails. On one occasion the quails settled deep and thick round the Israelites' camp. For two days and a night the people eagerly gathered up the birds and some of the people were greedy enough to over-eat. Those who were greedy were smitten with the plague as a punishment. *Numbers 11. 31–34.*

QUARTUS.   Paul mentions Quartus in his letter to the Romans. He was a member of

Rachel came with her father's sheep to the well and Jacob rolled back the stone —p. 135

the church in Corinth and his name means 'fourth' or 'quarter'. *Romans 16. 23.*

QUIRINIUS. Luke mentions this Roman governor who was the head of the Roman government in Syria. It was he who organized the numbering of the people, or the census, and he included Judaea in his area, which brought Mary and Joseph to Bethlehem. *Luke 2. 2.*

QUIVER. A leather case, made of skin, to hold arrows for the bowmen or archers. It was carried on the back. *Isaiah 22. 6.*

RABBAH (see also *Og*). The present day capital of Jordan, Amman, is said to be the site of Rabbah where Og, king of Bashan, had his huge iron bedstead. It was at Rabbah that David fought a famous battle against the Ammonites and made the people work for him in brick making and building. *2 Samuel 12. 26–31.*

RABBI, RABBONI. The Hebrew words for 'master' or 'teacher'. Jesus was often called 'rabbi'. The religious leaders of the Jewish people loved being called 'rabbi'. But Jesus warned his disciples against it. For them, God was the only teacher. Rabboni meant 'master' in a very special way. *Matthew 23. 7–9.*

RACA. A word in the Aramaic language which means 'scoundrel' or 'fool'. It was a strong, angry word and Jesus warned his disciples against using it. *Matthew 5. 22.*

RACHEL (see also *Jacob*). Jacob's wife, and mother of Joseph and Benjamin, a woman of great beauty. Jacob first saw her when she came to the well with her father's sheep. Jacob worked for fourteen years for Rachel's father Laban in order to have Rachel as wife. Rachel died soon after giving birth to Benjamin. Jacob raised a monument to her near Ramah about five miles north of Jerusalem. *Genesis 29. 17ff.*

RAHAB. Rahab lived in a house on the town wall of Jericho, and on its roof hid the two spies of Joshua's army. She made a secret arrangement with the spies. She let them escape through a window of her house on the wall. In return they agreed that Rahab should be saved when the city was captured by Joshua. She hung a red cord out of her window as a signal to the Israelite army. Later, Rahab and her family joined the Israelites. *Joshua 6. 22–25.*

RAIN. Rain is often mentioned in the Bible because the Bible lands are dry and hot. Rain was very welcome. There is a rainy season and a dry season. In October the rains that the Bible calls 'the former

A reminder of God's love to all men—the rainbow

rains' begin. Then in January the 'latter rains' start. Rain brought many blessings to men, the cattle, the land and the crops. *Psalm 72. 6; Amos 4. 7.*

RAINBOW. 'I set my bow in the cloud.' That was God's sign to Noah as the rain stopped and the waters of the great flood decreased. The word 'bow' means a 'bow' used in war. It was God's 'war-bow' seen in the heavens against the dark skies. The 'bow' then became lovely to look at in colour and sunlight, a reminder of God's love to all men.
Genesis 9. 13; Revelation 10. 1.

RAMAH. The birthplace of Samuel and his home from where he made his visits to the people of Judah. It was at Ramah that Saul first met Samuel, and David found refuge. The name means 'high' and Ramah was high in the hills north-west of Jerusalem. *1 Samuel 1. 19; 15. 34.*

RAMOTH-GILEAD. To the east of the Jordan in the hills of the land of Gad, Ramoth-Gilead was a walled city. It was often captured in the fighting between Israel and the Syrians. *Deuteronomy 4. 43.*

REBEKAH, REBECCA (see also *Isaac*). When Abraham sent his steward to look for a wife for Isaac he told him to go back to the lands in Mesopotamia where Abraham came from. With ten camels and many gifts the steward came to the well at Nahor, and there met Rebekah. She gave the 'servant water to drink for himself and his camels' and brought him to her family. Abraham's servant told the story of Abraham and his wish that his son Isaac should have a wife from his own country. Rebekah agreed to become his wife. Rebekah became the mother of Esau and Jacob. The Jewish people look on her as the mother of their race. *Genesis 24.*

RECHAB, RECHABITES. The descendants of Rechab refused to drink wine, and were commanded to live in tents, neither to sow nor plant, nor build houses. They were the Jewish groups who remembered the years of travel in the wilderness and sought to be like that always. Those were the days, they believed, when Israel was true to God, and the Rechabites looked back to that day. *Jeremiah 35. 2–10.*

A reed shaken in the wind

RED SEA. The sea that divides Africa and Arabia. It runs for 1200 miles from Aden to the southern tip of the Sinai Peninsula. There it divides into two big gulfs—the Gulf of Suez and the Gulf of Aqabah. The most famous Bible story about the Red Sea is the miraculous crossing of the sea by the Israelites on their flight from Egypt. No one knows exactly where they crossed, but most likely they crossed near the Bitter Lakes, or 'Sea of Reeds', which lies along the route of the modern Suez

Canal. There God sent a strong east wind which blew back the waters for the Israelites to cross dry-shod. But the Egyptians were trapped in the waters.
Exodus 14.

REED. Tall grasses often called 'rushes' which grew in marshy places and along river banks. Sometimes a reed grew as high as ten feet. It swayed in the wind and was blown about by the storms. It was not strong and easily buckled up.
1 Kings 14. 15; Matthew 11. 7.

The sea barrier which became a gateway for the Israelites

REFINER, REFINING. When a precious metal such as gold or silver needed to be cleaned, and made free from impurities, it was placed in a crucible or furnace made of clay and heated by a fire. The good metal came through the test of the fire, clean and refined, while the impurities fell away. The Bible describes this method as one of God's ways of dealing with people. Like a master-refiner God is always drawing out the pure metal in men's lives.
Psalm 12. 6; Isaiah 48. 10.

REHOBOAM. A son of King Solomon, and the first king of the southern kingdom of Judah. He reigned from 922–915 B.C., and the Bible says of him that 'he did not set his heart to seek the Lord.'
2 Chronicles 12. 13–14.

REPENTANCE. In the Bible the word repentance usually means 'to turn' or 'return'—to turn away from sin to God. This was the call of Jesus to the people in his day, and it was the call of the prophets in the Old Testament. To believe in God and to know that we are 'saved' through faith in him goes with repentance. We must turn away from sin and have faith in God's love and mercy.
Ezekiel 14. 6; Mark 1. 15.

REPHAIM. Some of the early inhabitants of the land of Palestine before the conquest by the Israelites. They were said to be giants in size. They lived chiefly to the east of the Jordan in the land of Moab.
Genesis 15. 20.

REPHIDIM. The last stopping place of the Israelites on their way out of Egypt before they reached Mount Sinai. There they fought the Amalekites. As Moses held up his hands in prayer they won; when he let them fall, they lost. So Aaron and Hur propped up the old man's hands and Joshua won a mighty victory. *Exodus 17. 8–16.*

RESURRECTION. The most wonderful thing about Jesus Christ as we read of him

137

'On the first day
of the week at
early dawn, they
went to the tomb...
and found the
stone rolled away'

in the Bible is the fact that he rose from the dead. He was crucified, he died and was buried. But when his disciples came to see his body in the tomb, it was not there. Some of the Jews said that his disciples had stolen the body away. But the disciples knew that Jesus had risen. They saw him after the Resurrection and they began to preach about Jesus as their risen Lord and Saviour. The Resurrection made the Christian faith quite different from any other religion. It gave the Christian church a faith that was wonderful to believe and even more wonderful to preach. It is the Resurrection of Jesus Christ from the dead that turns Christianity into a faith for all men to believe. The Resurrection makes it plain that this present life is not the end but only the beginning of a finer life in the world to come. *1 Corinthians 15. 12–19.*

REUBEN. The first born son of Jacob and the ancestor of the tribe of Reuben which came into the Promised Land and lived on the east side of Jordan. It was Reuben who advised his brothers not to kill Joseph their youngest brother and it was Reuben who went back to the pit to look for Joseph, and it was he who offered his own two sons as a guarantee for the safety of Benjamin. *Genesis 37. 29; 42. 37.*

REVELATION, BOOK OF. The last book of the Bible is full of pictures, descriptions and visions of the future glory of God's kingdom. Like the Book of Daniel in the Old Testament it points to the wonderful things that God can do, and it draws the reader away into another world. It was written, most likely, during the time when Christians were being persecuted and imprisoned by the Roman Emperors Nero and Domitian. The writer tells his Christian readers that Christ will come again in great glory, and that he will conquer all the powers of evil. He shows them in picture language the beauty and wonder of a new heaven and a new earth and is sure that God's way will always win the victory. *Book of Revelation.*

RHODA. The disciples were meeting in the house of John Mark's mother in Jerusalem. It was a sad meeting because Peter was in prison, and they wondered how he was faring. Suddenly a knock was heard at the door, and Rhoda, the maid in the house, ran to answer it. She heard a familiar voice at the doorway, and rushed back to the group and whispered excitedly, 'It's Peter.' They laughed and said, 'No. It can't be. He's in prison.' But Rhoda was sure and went to open the door, and brought Peter in. He described his wonderful escape from prison. *Acts 12. 12–17.*

RHODES. A large island on the sea route between Greece and the coast of Palestine. Paul called there on his last journey to Jerusalem. *Acts 21. 1.*

RIGHTEOUSNESS. One of the great words of the Bible which means right action, and fair dealing between man and man in all the affairs of life. The Hebrews thought of God as a 'righteous' God, one who wished to see the right things done. Jesus Christ showed God's righteousness in the best way of all by living it in his daily life. God continues to be 'righteous' towards men although they are sinful. It is God's love that helps men to practise 'right-doing' both towards God and towards men. *Amos 5. 24; Romans 3. 21ff.*

RIMMON. A god of the Syrians with a temple in the city of Damascus. He was the god of storm and war and was sometimes called 'The Thunderer'. Naaman, the Syrian general, was a worshipper of Rimmon. *2 Kings 5. 18–19.*

She ran to tell them it was Peter at the door

RIZPAH. Rizpah was the mother of Mephibosheth and Armoni, sons of King Saul. *2 Samuel 21. 8ff.*

ROCK. The Bible uses 'rock' to describe strength and security. Jesus Christ himself is described as the 'cornerstone' or 'rock' of God's church.
Psalm 118. 22; Romans 9. 33.

ROMANS, EPISTLE TO THE. The letter that Paul wrote to the Christians living in Rome is one of the finest he ever wrote. It is also one of his longest letters and is written with very great care. He probably wrote it during his stay in Greece about the year A.D. 58. Paul writes to the Christians in the great city of Rome about many of the deep truths he had learned about Christ and Christ's meaning for all human life. He writes about the 'righteousness' of God, the 'goodness' of God, the 'power' of God, the 'law' of God and the 'love' of God. In this great letter to the Christians in Rome we see deeply into the mind of Paul, and of the wonderful discoveries

Centre of the world in the days of Christ Rome provided Law, Government, Learning

he had made of God's love in Jesus Christ.
Epistle to the Romans

ROME. On its seven hills above the River Tiber, Rome was the capital of the world all during the life of Jesus Christ. From Rome the mighty Roman Empire spread into every country then on the map. It had over a million people in it. The buildings of Rome were many and magnificent, and travellers from all parts of the world came to the city. Paul was amongst the many who wished to see Rome. It is not known how Christianity started in Rome, or how Paul, and Peter, lived in the city. But there were many Christians in Rome during the first hundred years of Christian times, and being in the capital city the Roman Christians were always marked men. Many of them died for their faith in Jesus Christ.
Acts 19. 21; 28. 14ff.

RUBY. A precious jewel of shining red stone. It is mentioned six times in the Old Testament. Wisdom, says the Book of Proverbs, is more precious than rubies.
Proverbs 3. 15.

RUTH, BOOK OF (see also *Boaz, Naomi*). Ruth is the heroine of this rural story in the Old Testament, which bears her name. She lived in the land of Moab and there married one of the sons of Naomi, who had come from Bethlehem with her family in a time of famine. Ruth's husband died and there were no children. Her mother-in-law Naomi wished to go back to Bethlehem and Ruth decided to go with her. Naomi begged her to stay with her own people but Ruth refused to stay. In Bethlehem she received kindness at the hands of Boaz the farmer-kinsman of Naomi and eventually became his wife. It is a tale of friendship, kindness and human love. From Ruth's family in Bethlehem David came and so the Book of Ruth has a direct link with the family of Jesus.
Book of Ruth.

S SABBATH. In the Bible the law is laid down that one day in seven is to be observed as a day holy to God—a day on which work ceases. The Hebrew word 'sabbath' means 'to cease'. The Fourth

Commandment is a reminder of this law. The Old Testament gives many instructions about the keeping of the Sabbath and the Jewish people were very particular in obeying them. But Jesus pointed out that the Sabbath was a day to be used for God's worship and work, and that work done on the Sabbath in God's name did not spoil the holy day. The early Christians observed

takes many different forms. Sometimes a 'gift' is offered to God to express joy and thanksgiving, or to seal a treaty between two men. In other cases the aim of sacrifice is to show repentance for a sin committed. The materials for the sacrifice had to be the best obtainable, either a living animal or the produce of the earth. The Old Testament had exact regulations about the time, place, and method of the sacrifice and about the part played by the worshipper and the priest. In the New Testament Jesus did not despise the Old Testament sacrifices, but he thought of them as belonging to the 'old way'. He pointed to himself as greater than the Temple and its sacrifices. He was the founder of the 'new way', with himself

Bullock, sheep, goat and pigeon were all used in sacrifice

their 'Sabbath' on the first day of the week, the day on which Jesus rose from the dead, and called it the 'Lord's Day'.
Exodus 20. 8; Mark 1. 23ff; Luke 13. 10–17.

SACKCLOTH. A cloth usually made of black goat's hair, and very coarse. It was worn at a time of mourning, or national disaster, or when the wearer wished to show penitence. The piece of sackcloth was sometimes tied round the waist, or worn next to the skin.
1 Kings 20. 31; Matthew 11. 21.

SACRIFICE. The offering of sacrifice to the gods is a common practice amongst primitive peoples. In the Old Testament it

as High Priest entering his Father's presence and preparing a way for us to follow.
1 Samuel 15. 14; Hebrews 10.

SADDUCEES. The word Sadducees stands for those men in the Bible who were descendants of the priest Zadok to whom was given the right of officiating in the Temple. They were the 'priestly party' and became the enemies of Jesus when he interfered in the affairs of the Temple by driving out the merchants and the money-changers. They dominated the high council of the Jews, the Sanhedrin, and were on the conservative side of the Jewish faith seeking to preserve its ancient ways, traditions, and laws. *Matthew 22. 23 ff.*

SALAMIS. A town on the east coast of Cyprus where Paul and Barnabas preached in the synagogues. *Acts 13. 5.*

SALEM. An ancient name for Jerusalem, the city of Salem, meaning 'safe, at peace'. *Hebrews 7. 1–2.*

SALOME. Salome was one of the three women who went to the tomb of Jesus on Easter morning. She was the mother of James and John, the sons of Zebedee. Salome may also have been the sister of Mary the mother of Jesus, which would make James and John cousins of Jesus. *Mark 15. 40.*

SALT. Salt was valued in Bible times, as it is today, as a preservative and for seasoning food. It was also a symbol of truth and loyalty. The Hebrew people had ample supplies of salt from the region of the Salt (or Dead) Sea, and from the neighbouring Hill of Salt and Valley of Salt. Sometimes the outer layers of this 'rock salt' lacked salty flavour and had to be thrown away as Jesus described in one of his parables. *Leviticus 2. 13; Matthew 5. 13.*

SALVATION, SAVIOUR, These great biblical words mean 'to save' and to give 'health'. They suggest 'safety', and 'prosperity', and also 'moral' and 'spiritual' deliverance. The Bible tells the story of man's 'salvation', of the 'deliverance' from his old self into a new state of life through the action of God. The 'plan of salvation' begins in the Old Testament and unfolds itself fully in the New Testament in 'the person of Jesus Christ the Saviour'. It is Jesus who 'saves' men from their sins. In him the holy love of God is shown supremely in his death on the Cross. There we are united with him in victory over sin. By his love towards God and love towards men Christ performs the 'saving' act and makes peace between God and men. *Psalm 68. 19ff; Luke 2. 11; Romans 1. 16.*

SAMARIA, SAMARITANS. The name of the northern section of Israel whose city of Samaria was built on a hill overlooking the great plain of Esdraelon by King Omri in 876 B.C. Many of the Israelite kings lived in Samaria which was often attacked by the Syrians. In 721 B.C. the Assyrians captured Samaria and thousands of its people were

Salome was amongst the women who followed Jesus from Galilee

carried off into captivity. There was hatred between the people of Judah in the south and the Samaritans in the north who were a mixed race and were thought not to be wholly loyal to Israel's God. The Samaritans built their own Temple on Mount Gerizim, which deeply offended the Jews, and the barriers between the two peoples were very strong. The Samaritans today are a small community of about three hundred people living at Nablus. They hold in the main to

Jewish beliefs and customs, but believe that Mount Gerizim is the place appointed by God for worship.

1 Kings 16. 24; John 4. 1–40.

SAMSON. Before he was born Samson was dedicated to God as a Nazarite. He became a 'prophet' and a 'judge'. He was famous for his feats of physical strength, and for his hatred of the Philistines. He once caught 300 jackals, tied firebrands to their tails and turned them loose in the grainfields of the Philistines and burned the crops. With the jawbone of an ass he fought a whole Philistine army. Those mighty acts gave him authority in his own land of

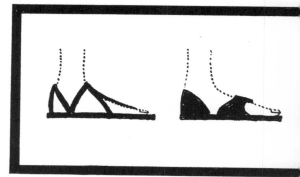

Judah. But his immoral association with Delilah led to his downfall. She discovered that his hair was the secret of his strength and cut it and then betrayed him to the Philistines who captured and blinded him. He was put to hard labour in Gaza and exhibited at a feast for the god Dagon. His hair had grown and his strength came back. At the feast he pulled down the wooden pillars of the portico from which thousands of spectators were watching him. The pillars crashed down killing the chief people of the land, and Samson as well. By his death Samson won a great victory over the Philistines. *Judges 13–16.*

SAMUEL (see also *Eli, Hannah*). 'And the Lord called, Samuel, Samuel, and he answered, Here am I.' In the darkness of the Temple at night God spoke to the

'Then Samson bowed with all his might and the house fell'

young serving boy who assisted the aged priest Eli. Three times the call came until Eli was convinced that it was God himself speaking to the boy. That was the beginning of the career of Samuel, one of the great men of the Old Testament who was the last of the judges and the first of the prophets. It was Samuel who helped to establish the kingship in Israel, and chose King Saul and King David. It was Samuel's wisdom and sensitive response to God which were always ready to be of service to the people. He was a 'kingmaker' but also aware of the God who was greater than any earthly king. *1 Samuel 3.*

they planned to re-build the walls of Jerusalem but Sanballat came to oppose the plan, and by various tricks tried to stop Nehemiah's builders; probably out of jealousy as a man of Samaria against a leader of the Jews. *Nehemiah 6. 1–9.*

SANCTIFICATION, SANCTIFY. As the Bible uses these words they mean 'holy' and 'to make holy'. The Old Testament sees God as a 'holy God' and the people are expected to be 'holy'—or 'set apart' towards him. They do this by many outward ceremonial observances. In the New Testament the two words are more closely related to a change in the life of the Christian

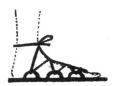

Sandals for the road, but never in the house

SAMUEL, BOOKS OF. The two books of Samuel are part of the 'history books' of Israel and tell the story of how Israel moved from the government of 'judges' to that of 'kings'. It contains some of the finest narrative history in the Bible—the career of Samuel, the call of Saul and David to the kingship, the David and Goliath episode, the friendship of David and Jonathan, the wanderings of David and the establishment of his kingship and capital in Jerusalem. The two books record much that is evil but also much that is noble in the life of Israel and in the people's understanding of the one true God. *Books of Samuel.*

SANBALLAT. Sanballat was governor of Samaria at the time when some of the Jewish people came back from captivity in Persia in 445 B.C. Under Nehemiah

believer who is 'sanctified' or made 'holy' by faith in Christ.
Joshua 7.13; John 17. 17.

SANCTUARY. A 'sanctuary' is a place set apart for the worship of God. The first 'sanctuary' that the people of Israel knew was the movable tent, the 'tabernacle' which housed the Ark of the Covenant. After many years, when they were settled in the Land of Promise, a great temple was built by Solomon which became the official 'sanctuary' of Hebrew worship.
1 Chronicles 22. 19; Psalm 96. 6.

SANDAL (see also *Latchet*). The sandal was regular footwear in Bible times—except for poor people who walked in bare feet. The soles of the sandal were usually made of leather or wood and tied with leather thongs. *Mark 1. 7.*

SANHEDRIN. The name of the highest Jewish court, or council. It started under Moses as a council of seventy elders to assist him in governing the people. In the days of Jesus, the Sanhedrin consisted of the high priest, and those who had been high priests, members of privileged families, the heads of the tribes and members of the two parties —the Sadducees and the Pharisees. *Numbers 11. 16; Mark 15.*

SARDIS. One of the 'seven churches of Asia' mentioned in the Book of Revelation. Under Croesus it had become a by-word for riches and it rested on its famous reputation. The Christian church in the city was also a bit like that. It was failing to 'keep awake' and was threatened with spiritual death. *Revelation 3. 1–6.*

SATAN. A Hebrew word which means *adversary*, and is used as a name for the chief

'David took the lyre and played it, so Saul was refreshed, and was well'

of evil spirits, or the devil. The New Testament thinks of Satan as the one who is always working against God. The New Testament sees a great battle in progress between God and Satan. Jesus was 'tempted of Satan' to make wrong decisions at the beginning of his ministry, and on other occasions too Jesus had to 'rebuke' Satan. Satan continues to tempt men and to hinder God's work in their hearts. But the New Testament is sure that in the end God will triumph over evil.
Matthew 4. 1–11; Acts 5. 3.

SAUL. The first king of Israel, in 1020 B.C. His story takes up most of the first Book of Samuel. A man of courage, good physique and character, he seemed to be the right kind of man to be king. Samuel's choice of Saul appeared at first to be a good one. Saul defeated the Ammonites and refused to massacre all his enemies. But Saul soon became disobedient to the laws of God. He refused to listen to Samuel's advice. He failed as king because he did not understand his relationship to God as well as to the people, and was never master of his own moodiness and selfishness. God, through the prophet Samuel, rejected him as king.
First Book of Samuel.

SCEPTRE. A decorated or carved rod, or staff, carried in front of a king, or a ruler, to signify his authority. Christ is described in the New Testament as having the 'sceptre' of the kingdom of righteousness.
Psalm 45. 6; Hebrews 1. 8.

SCHOOL. Schools are not mentioned much in the Bible. Moses was commanded to teach the people the law, and in the time of the 'prophets' in Israel young men were instructed by them at the local places of worship. In the New Testament the word 'school' occurs only once. The 'Synagogue' was the real school for all Jewish children.
John 18. 20; Acts 19. 9.

SCHOOLMASTER. The Roman and Greek schoolmaster was a slave who generally looked after the boy and took him to school and not one who taught him. Paul speaks of 'the law' as 'the schoolmaster' who brings us to Christ.
Galatians 3. 24–25.

SCRIBE. In eastern countries, including Israel, the scribe, the man who could write, was an important person. Scribes were employed by the kings and rulers, and sometimes became advisers and administrators. The scribe carried his pen-case and ink-horn hanging from his girdle. He also had a reed-pen, and a knife for corrections and cutting papyrus.
2 Kings 22. 8; Ezra 4. 8.

SCRIBES. The Scribes were the lawyers, the experts on the Law of Moses. In the days of Jesus the Scribes were the professional defenders of the law, and knew all the legal traditions associated with the law, and were eager to see that everyone obeyed it. It was this over-zealous attention to the law that Jesus objected to. The Scribes were opposed to Jesus because he spoke as one who was above the law and had his own authority. *Matthew 7. 29; Acts 6. 12.*

Scrip for the journey? Never go without it

SCRIP. A little bag or wallet for carrying food, usually made of animal skin and slung from the shoulder by straps.
1 Samuel 17. 40; Matthew 10. 10.

A cylinder seal
rolled on clay

SCRIPTURE. The word means a 'writing' and the Bible uses it to refer to the sacred writings we know as the Old Testament. At some unknown time Christians also began to refer to their own 'writings', such as the Gospels and Paul's letters, as 'scripture'. It may be that even in Paul's lifetime certain 'words' of Jesus may have been linked with the Old Testament and referred to as 'scripture'. *1 Corinthians 15. 3.*

Scroll—perhaps
a goat or sheep
skin

SCROLL, DEAD SEA SCROLLS. In Bible times a book consisted of a roll or scroll of papyrus or parchment. The text was written on the front and back of the scroll. Sometimes a scroll was called the 'roll of a book'.

The Dead Sea Scrolls were discovered in 1947 in caves at Qumran near the Dead Sea. Among the scrolls were copies of parts of the Old Testament. A search was made through eleven of the caves and five hundred documents were discovered which had been well preserved in the clear, dry air of the Dead Sea area. These documents were part of the library of a community which flourished at Qumran for two hundred years up to about A.D. 70. It was a strict Jewish religious community which hoped for the coming of a 'Teacher of Righteousness'. It may be that some of its members joined the early Christian church in Jerusalem. When they were forced by war to leave their Dead Sea home, the community stored their library of parchment scrolls in the caves. The scrolls have helped scholars to know the Old Testament writings much better, and have also provided fresh knowledge of the New Testament background. *Ezekiel 2. 9–10.*

SCYTHIAN. A tribe of horse-riding nomads who lived in the Black Sea–Caspian area. Paul refers to 'Scythian' in his letter to the Colossians. In his day they were probably settled as traders in the region. *Colossians 3. 11.*

SEAL. In the days when few people could read or write a seal fixed to a document was like a signature. It was a sign of its truth and authority. Some seals were specially engraved on a precious stone, and then the seal was stamped in wax, or a clay lump on the papyrus. Seals were sometimes set in a ring for the finger, or hung round the neck. *1 Kings 21. 8.*

SEIR. A region in the land of Edom inhabited by the descendants of Esau who conquered its original inhabitants. *Genesis 14. 6.*

SELAH. This word occurs some seventy times in the Psalms and is thought to be a musical sign perhaps as an indication to the singers to 'pause' or 'sing up'. Or it may have been a sign to lift up the voice or hands in prayer in public worship. *Book of Psalms.*

SELEUCIA. The port on the coast of Syria from where Paul and Barnabas sailed after they had been commissioned by the church at Antioch on their first missionary journey. *Acts 13. 4.*

SENNACHERIB. The king of Assyria from 705–681 B.C. He fought Hezekiah, king of Judah, who had to pay great sums of money to him. But Hezekiah later fought back and won a great victory over the

The sepulchre was often cut deep in the rock

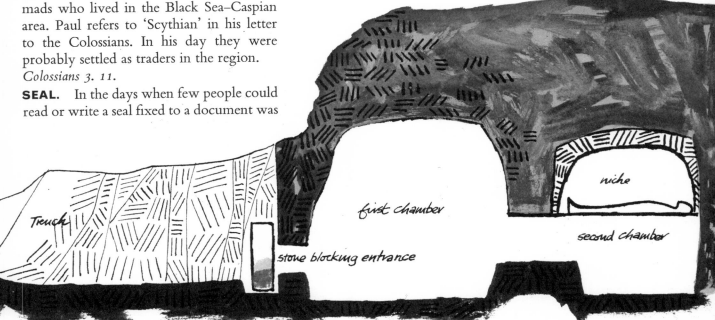

Trench

stone blocking entrance

first chamber

niche

second chamber

Assyrians. Sennacherib re-built Nineveh as his capital city and extended his empire over vast areas, now modern Iran and Iraq. *2 Kings 18–19.*

SEPULCHRE, TOMB. The Hebrews buried their dead in caverns or caves cut out of cliffs called sepulchres. The entrance to the chamber was closed by a stone to keep animals out. The sepulchres were in lonely places outside the towns and sometimes there were shelves for a number of bodies. Except by wealthy people coffins were not used. It was customary to whitewash the outside of the sepulchre so that it could be clearly seen and to prevent anyone touching it becoming 'unclean'. This led Jesus to call the Pharisees 'whited sepulchres' or 'whitewashed tombs'—clean outside and foul within. *Matthew 23. 27.*

SERAPHIM (see also *Cherubim*). The heavenly beings who with the Cherubim guarded the divine throne. As described in the vision of Isaiah they each had six wings, and led in divine worship by calling to one another, 'Holy, holy, holy is the Lord of hosts.' One of the seraphim flew to Isaiah carrying a burning coal from the altar, touched his lips and made him clean and fit to be a prophet of God. *Isaiah 6. 1–7.*

SERGIUS PAULUS. The Roman governor of Cyprus when the apostle Paul visited the island. He listened to the preaching of Paul and Barnabas, and some believe that he became a Christian. *Acts 13. 7–12.*

SERMON ON THE MOUNT. 'And seeing the multitudes he went up into a mountain, and he opened his mouth and taught them.' So begins the fifth chapter of Matthew's Gospel and what is traditionally called 'The Sermon on the Mount.' This 'sermon' extends to chapter seven and is actually a collection of the teachings and sayings of Jesus about the character and purpose of the kingdom of God. It begins with the Beatitudes, and also, in parable and story, gives much practical instruction in living the Christian life. While the 'sermon' was preached to the people yet it is aimed specially at the disciples. It speaks of the conduct and character of those within the kingdom of God. *Matthew 5–7.*

SERPENT, BRAZEN. 'Moses made a bronze serpent and set it on a pole.' That act of Moses as the people of Israel crossed the Sinai wilderness to the borders of the Promised Land was by direct order from God. The people were suffering from deadly snake bites and asked Moses to save them from these pests. 'Everyone who looks at the serpent on the pole shall live' came the reply. It was a dramatic way of showing the power of God, and of the deliverance from evil that would come through obedience to him. No wonder the people later tried to turn the 'brazen serpent' into an idol, and it had to be destroyed.
Numbers 21. 6–9.

SERVANT OF THE LORD. In the Bible a 'servant' means someone who works for a master. It was also used for slaves in the service of the king. The Old Testament often thinks of Israel as the 'servant of the Lord', and in the Book of Isaiah there are the 'Servant Songs' which refer to Israel but also remind us of Jesus. Often Jesus referred to himself as 'servant', as one who serves God in the spirit of humility and suffering.
Isaiah 49ff; Mark 10. 45; Philippians 2. 7.

SETH. The third son of Adam and Eve born after the murder of Abel and called Seth which means 'appointed'.
Genesis 4. 25.

SEVEN WORDS, THE. The words which Christ spoke from the Cross are often grouped together as the 'Seven Words'. *First* to the Roman soldiers; *second* to the penitent thief; *third* to his mother; *fourth* to God his Father; *fifth* 'I thirst'; *sixth* 'it is finished'; *seventh* to his Father.
Luke 23. 34; 43; John 19. 25–27; Matthew 27. 46; John 19. 28; 30; Luke 23. 46.

SHADRACH—see *Abednego* and *Meshach*.

SHAMGAR. One of the warriors of Israel in their warfare with the Philistines. He killed 600 Philistines with a metal ox goad.
Judges 3. 31; 5. 6.

SHAPHAN (see also *Josiah*). The scribe and secretary to King Josiah who reported to him the discovery of the Book of the Law in the Temple. *2 Kings 22. 3.*

'You are to be merciful, pure in heart and peacemakers'

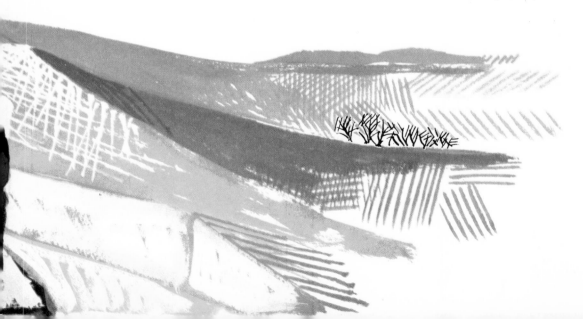

SHARON. The Plain of Sharon lies along the Mediterranean shore of Israel roughly from Joppa to Mount Carmel. It is about fifty miles long and ten miles wide. It was famous for its forests, and is now one of the rich agricultural areas of Israel with orange groves and farm lands.
Isaiah 35. 2.

SHEBA, QUEEN OF. The fame of King Solomon, his riches and wisdom spread far and wide and many visitors came to Jerusalem. One of them was the 'Queen of Sheba' from the area of Saba in south-west Arabia. She came with her camel train over 1200 miles to Jerusalem with presents of gold and spices and precious stones. She put 'hard questions' to Solomon, and was astonished not only at his answers but at the splendour and luxury of his court. 'I did not believe the reports until I came,' she said, 'and behold, the half was not told me.'
1 Kings 10. 1–10.

SHECHEM. An important town in Samaria with a long history stretching back to the days of Abraham. When the Israelites conquered Palestine, Shechem was a rallying point to the people, and it was for a time the capital of Samaria and became the chief city of the Samaritans. Many excavations have been made at Shechem during the last fifty years. *Joshua 24.*

SHEKEL. A weight or coin which differed according to times and places. A famous measurement was the weight in bronze of Goliath's armour, 5000 shekels or about 125 pounds. The silver shekel was a coin worth about 3s. 9d. or 66 cents, or, in gold, two pounds or about six dollars.
Genesis 23. 15; 24. 22; 1 Samuel 17. 5.

SHEM. The eldest son of Noah and the ancestor of the people mentioned in the Book of Genesis, some of whom spoke the 'Semitic' languages such as Hebrew.
Genesis 10. 21–31.

SHEPHERD. The Bible speaks of two kinds of shepherd—the one who cares for

The Shepherd calleth his own sheep by name

sheep and the other who 'shepherds' human beings. The picture of the shepherd devoted to the care of his flock, leading them to pasture and water and seeking any which are lost, is strongly and vividly painted in the Bible. God himself is thought of as the Shepherd of Israel, and Jesus spoke of himself as the Good Shepherd ready to lay down his own life for the sake of his sheep. *Psalm 23; John 10. 1–18.*

SHIBBOLETH. A 'catch-word' or 'test-word' used when defeated Ephraimites tried to escape across Jordan. Each prisoner was asked to pronounce *shibboleth.* If he said *sibboleth* he was known to be an Ephraimite and was killed. The word nowadays often stands for the cheap 'catch-word' or 'slogan' of a sect or party. *Judges 12. 5–6.*

SHILOH. About nine miles to the north of Bethel, Shiloh was one of the main sanctuaries of the Israelites during the time of the Judges. Samuel's parents used to go every year to worship at Shiloh. *1 Samuel 1. 3.*

SHINAR. Another name for the great plain in which the city of Babylon was built and where the Tower of Babel was erected. *Isaiah 11. 11.*

SHIP. The Hebrews were not a seafaring people, but there are many references to ships in the Bible. King Solomon had his own sea-going fleet of ships, probably rowed by galley slaves. The ships that Jesus knew were the fishing boats on the Sea of Galilee, which depended on oars, but also had sails. The ships Paul sailed in were small coastal vessels, but on his journey to Rome he sailed in two of the great sailing ships that carried grain from Egypt to Italy. *1 Kings 9. 26; Psalm 107. 23; Acts 27.*

SHISHAK. The king of Egypt, who in the year 918 B.C. invaded Palestine with 1,200 chariots and 60,000 horsemen, and captured King Rehoboam. *1 Kings 14. 25–28.*

SHITTIM. The last camping place of the Israelites entering Canaan. From Shittim Joshua sent out his spies to Jericho. Shittim was in Moab, east of the Jordan, and was famous for its acacia trees (shittim wood) of which the Ark of the Covenant was made. *Exodus 25. 10; Joshua 2. 1.*

SHOWBREAD. The twelve baked cakes made of fine flour which were placed freshly every Sabbath on a table of gold in the holy place of the Tabernacle. It was the bread of 'the presence of God.' The showbread was a reminder to the Israelites of how God had provided for them in the wilderness and was still the provider of life and food. It was showbread that David was given to eat by the priest Abimelech when no other bread was available for the hungry men. *Leviticus 24. 5–9; 1 Samuel 21. 3–6; Matthew 12. 3–4.*

SHUSHAN, SUSA. One of the capital cities of ancient Persia. King Darius built his palace there and the story of Esther and King Ahasuerus is set in Susa. *Esther 1. 2.*

SIDON. The ancient port and city in the Lebanon often captured and re-captured in over a thousand years of stormy history. In the days of Jesus it was an independent city under the Romans. Many people of Sidon listened to the teachings of Jesus, and it was in the neighbourhood of Sidon that he healed the daughter of the Greek woman. *Mark 3. 8.*

SILAS. In the church in Jerusalem Silas was a leading member. He was sent from Jerusalem to Antioch to welcome the Gentile Christians, and on Paul's second missionary journey Silas went with him. As a Roman citizen Silas had good standing and he seems to have been a generally useful person. *Acts 15. 36–41.*

SILOAM, POOL OF. 'Go, wash in the Pool of Siloam.' That was the command of

Showbread—a sign of God's goodness and provision

Jesus to the man born blind, after he had touched his eyes. Near the Fountain Gate in Jerusalem this Pool was part of the Jerusalem water system which King Hezekiah devised to bring water inside the city walls. It was traditional for sick people to bathe in its waters. *John 9. 7.*

SIMEON. 'Lord, now lettest thou thy servant depart in peace, according to thy word.' So spoke Simeon in the Temple on seeing the infant Jesus presented by his parents. His first two words are known in Latin as the *Nunc Dimittis.* Simeon is also the name of the second son of Jacob and Leah, and of one of the tribes of Israel. *Genesis 29. 33; Luke 2. 25–32.*

SIMON. Nine different people in the New Testament are called 'Simon'—Peter the chief disciple; Simon the Canaanite; Simon a brother of Jesus; Simon a leper in Bethany; Simon of Cyrene; Simon a Pharisee; Simon father of Judas Iscariot; Simon Magus; Simon the tanner of Joppa.
Matthew 4. 18; 10. 4; 13. 55; 26. 6; 27. 32; Luke 7. 40; John 6. 71; Acts 8. 9; 9. 43.

SIMON MAGUS. A magician of the 'city of Samaria' who became a Christian and imagined that he too could have the power that the apostles had if he gave them money. He was sternly rebuked by Peter, and asked for forgiveness. His later career (not recorded in the Bible) suggests that he never fully understood the Christian faith and was one of the first 'heretics'. *Acts 8. 9–24.*

SIN. The Bible uses the word 'sin' for wrong-doing, failure, error, or unrighteousness. 'Sin' is that which is directed against God. The first sin of Adam showed how man rebelled against the authority, goodness and wisdom of God. It also showed what the Bible calls the 'wrath' of God towards sin which is more than 'anger' against sin, because sin is an act against the character of God. All men are linked to Adam in 'sin', but can also be linked in 'forgiveness' to Christ who gives his life for sinful men. *Romans 5. 12–21.*

SIN, WILDERNESS OF. A sandy tract in the south-west corner of the Sinai peninsula through which the Israelites passed on their way to Mount Sinai. *Exodus 16. 1.*

SINAI, MOUNT. The exact location of the Mount Sinai of the Bible is uncertain, but the mountain of Gebel Musa (7303 feet) in the Sinai Peninsula is usually considered to be Mount Sinai. Here Moses received the Covenant between God and the Israelite people. There God revealed himself to Moses, and gave the Ten Commandments and other laws. At Mount Sinai the wandering Israelite tribesmen were bound together as a 'nation', and began to understand their role as the 'people of God'.
Exodus 19. 16–25.

SISERA (see also *Jael*). A general of the Canaanites who commanded Jabin's army against the people of Israel under Deborah and Barak and was treacherously killed by Jael. *Judges 4. 17–22.*

SLAVE, SLAVERY. In the Old Testament 'slaves' were those people who were in the control of others and did not have full rights over their own lives. Sometimes they were captured in war, or purchased as in the case of Joseph. They might be children born to 'slave-parents', or children who were sold to pay debts, or people who were stolen, or even those who sold themselves into slavery on account of poverty. The Old Testament shows that this kind of 'slavery' had its own laws and regulations about prices, conditions and treatment of slaves. These rights had to be respected. Jewish 'slavery' was humane and not cruel. 'Slavery' in the New Testament was Roman in its methods, and the slave was the property of his master who could do with him as he wished. But Bible teaching about God's love for all people has made men see how wrong slavery is.
Exodus 21. 1–6; Ephesians 6. 5–9.

SMYRNA. One of the 'seven churches' of Asia, now in Turkey. It was a prosperous port in New Testament times, and the Gospel came to it very early. In this commercial city the Christians were open to many temptations, and there were disputes between Jews and Christians. The message to the church is 'Be faithful and I will give you the crown of life.'
Revelation 2. 8–11.

SNARE. A device for catching birds or animals, usually a baited trap which caught the animal. *Psalm 124. 7.*

SODOM (see also *Gomorrah*). One of the 'cities of the plain' at the southern tip of the Dead Sea. Its wickedness was proverbial in Bible times and has remained so.
Genesis 18. 16–21.

SOLOMON. The king of all Israel, and son of David and Bathsheba, who reigned from 961 to 922 B.C. In spite of many short-comings his fame and achievements outstrip all the kings we read of in the Bible. He created a strong central government, overcoming the tribal divisions of the nation; he extended Israel's trade with surrounding countries, kept a strong army and was on friendly terms with neighbouring monarchs. He built the Temple in Jerusalem, making it a wonderful building for the Jewish people, and he collected some of the 'wise sayings' which are in the Book of Proverbs, part of the Wisdom Literature of the Israelites. His own fame as a wise man spread round the world, and his forty years' reign is a 'golden age' in the story of Israel. *1 Kings 3. 1–11.*

What do you do with your talents? Do you improve them or bury them? (see Matthew 25. 14)

SOLOMON, SONG OF. A collection of love poems sometimes called the Song of Songs, or Canticles, and by tradition attributed to Solomon. It describes human love in beautiful poetic language and illustrates its delights and wonders. These poems on the purity of human love also remind the Bible reader of the love of God which is even more wonderful. *Song of Solomon.*

SOSTHENES (see also *Crispus*). The chief ruler of the synagogue at Corinth and one who was associated with the converted Crispus. He too may have become a Christian. *Acts 18. 17.*

Saul of Tarsus was there at the stoning of Stephen

SPICES. Sweet smelling spices such as cinnamon, myrrh, mint, aloes and spikenard were much used in Bible times. Spices were brought by traders from Egypt, India and Mesopotamia, and were used to flavour wine and food and for the burning of incense in worship. When bodies were buried spices were placed in the grave clothes. *2 Chronicles 16. 14; Mark 16. 1.*

SPIKENARD. A fragrant oil made from the roots of the spikenard plant, which grows chiefly in North India. In Bible times spikenard was imported into Palestine in alabaster boxes and used for perfuming or anointing on special occasions. *John 12. 3.*

SPIRIT (see also *Holy Spirit*). In the Old Testament the word spirit (or *ruah*) occurs 378 times and is thought of as that which gives life and movement. It often means the 'wind' or 'breath' and refers to the 'spirit of God'. In the New Testament, spirit (or *pneuma*) appears 220 times and often means 'Holy Spirit', or 'divine spirit', and is directly linked with Christ. *Genesis 1. 2; Mark 1. 12; 2 Corinthians 3. 3.*

STEPHANAS. A member of the church in Corinth baptized by Paul and well known for Christian service. Paul was delighted that Stephanas took the trouble to visit him in Ephesus. *1 Corinthians 16. 15.*

STEPHEN. One of the seven 'deacons' chosen by the disciples in the very early days of the church to look after the practical affairs of the Christians in Jerusalem. Stephen's public preaching of the new faith roused the anger of the Jewish Council because he denounced them for failing to keep the law; for rejecting Jesus as the Christ, and for resisting the Holy Spirit. He was stoned to death. One of those who watched his courageous end was Saul of Tarsus who himself was soon to become a Christian. *Acts 7.*

STEWARD. In the Bible, the 'steward' is the man who manages the 'house'; the one who is the guardian of its affairs. It applies to all Christians too who are 'stewards' of Christ's affairs within Christ's house, the church. *Genesis 43. 19; 1 Corinthians 4. 1–2.*

STONING. This was the usual Hebrew form of executing a man who had been convicted of a crime worthy of death. Two witnesses for the prosecution had to throw the first stone. *Deuteronomy 13. 9–10; Luke 20. 6.*

STRANGER. This word is used in the Bible to cover a number of meanings. A 'stranger' is one who is an outsider, someone who does not belong to the local community. It can also mean a 'foreigner' of another race, or one who has come on a visit for a short time, a 'sojourner' who must be treated with every consideration. *Genesis 15. 13; Jeremiah 5. 19; Deuteronomy 10. 18–19.*

SUCCOTH. The first stop of the people of Israel on their way out of Egypt, and also the name given to a town of the tribe of Gad in the Jordan Valley. *Exodus 12. 37; Joshua 13. 27.*

SYCHAR. A town in Samaria mentioned only once in the Bible. Near Sychar Jesus met the woman of Samaria and talked about problems in her life and about the meaning of the worship of God. Some scholars identify Sychar with ancient Shechem. *John 4. 5.*

SYCAMORE. 'So he ran on ahead and climbed up into a sycamore tree' is Luke's description of how Zacchaeus managed to get a good look at Jesus. There amongst the spreading branches and the evergreen leaves Zacchaeus made up for his lack of inches and could see over the heads of the crowd. The sycamore tree of Egypt and Palestine grows to a height of 30–40 feet and grows very eatable figs. *1 Chronicles 27. 28; Luke 19. 4.*

SYNAGOGUE. The Jewish place of worship. The word means 'to meet together'. Before they were carried off to captivity in Babylon the Jews centred their worship on the Jerusalem Temple. But when that was impossible they began to form synagogues where the scriptures were read and prayer was offered. Synagogues existed wherever Jews lived. In the synagogue was the ark in which the scrolls of the Law and the Prophets were kept. Each synagogue had its own government with a chief officer or ruler and elders. The Sabbath was the appointed day for worship in the synagogue and at least ten adult men had to be present. The reading from the Scriptures was the most important event and a sermon was preached from the Prophets. In New Testament times every Jewish boy attended the synagogue for instruction in the Law and Scriptures. *Matthew 13. 54.*

SYRACUSE. On the last stage of his journey to Rome Paul's ship called at Syracuse, a port on the east coast of Sicily, whose history goes back to seven hundred years before Christ. *Acts 28. 12.*

SYRIA. The ancient kingdom of Syria lay to the north-east of Palestine. Three hundred years before Christ it stretched from the Mediterranean Sea to the borders of India, and for a period included Palestine itself. In the days of Jesus Syria was a small Roman province more roughly corresponding to the modern country of Syria. *Isaiah 7. 8; Acts 15. 23.*

T **TABERNACLE.** The Tabernacle was the portable 'tent' for the worship of God which the Israelites carried with them in their desert wanderings. It had two compartments. In one of them stood the Ark of the Covenant made of gold; in the other were the incense altar, the showbread table and the lampstand. Solomon brought the 'tabernacle' into the Jerusalem Temple and also put the ark in its new place. *Exodus 26. 1; 1 Kings 8. 1–16.*

TABERNACLES, FEAST OF. One of the three great festivals of the Jewish Year. It was kept for seven days at the time of the year when the harvest was over. Little booths of leaves and branches of trees were erected on the farms and the people were required to live in them for seven days. This feast reminded the Jews of their days of wandering in the desert and the temporary homes they had to make. *Leviticus 23. 39–43.*

TABOR, MOUNT. An isolated hill which rises above the Plain of Esdraelon to 1843 feet above sea-level, with steep slopes and a rounded top. Traditionally said to be the 'Mount of Transfiguration' (but see Hermon.) *Psalm 89. 12.*

TALENT. The 'talent' was not a single coin but a measure in reckoning money.

The
**sycamore
spread its
branches and
leaves in
graceful style
(see Zacchaeus)**

It was always of high value and varied according to the weight of the metal, gold or silver. Jesus mentions the 'talent' in two parables. It was probably worth about a thousand dollars or three hundred and fifty pounds. *Matthew 18. 24; 25. 14–30.*

TALITHA CUMI (see also *Jairus*). 'Damsel arise'—the words spoken by Jesus to the daughter of Jairus. In the Aramaic tongue Jesus spoke the word 'damsel' is an affectionate word like 'lamb' or 'lambkin'. *Mark 5. 41.*

TARES. A Bible word for any kind of 'weed'. The 'bearded darnel' weed looked very much like wheat but at harvest time the two could easily be distinguished, and could be separated. *Matthew 13. 26–30.*

TARSHISH. The ships of Tarshish are often mentioned in the Old Testament, but where exactly was Tarshish? It must have been a land bordering the sea. Jonah set sail in a ship going to Tarshish. It was also a land with mines and minerals and many scholars believe that Spain is the land of Tarshish. *2 Chronicles 20. 36.*

TARSUS. Famous as the birthplace of Paul, Tarsus in the south of Asia Minor was a meeting place of east and west, Greeks, Romans and Jews. The Romans established themselves in the area about sixty years before Christ. They gave Roman citizenship to the Jews of the city. *Acts 21. 39.*

TEKOA. The home of the prophet Amos, a country town six miles south of Bethlehem. *Amos 1. 1.*

TEMPLE. After the people of Israel had settled in the Promised Land they needed a central, permanent shrine of worship which King David planned and his son Solomon built. It was a splendid and spacious building on which Solomon lavished much skill and treasure. It served the Jewish people as the central shrine of their worship from about 940 B.C. to 587 B.C. Returning from exile the Jews built a second temple which lasted for 500 years, and then in 19 B.C. King Herod began to build his 'temple' as a way of commending himself to the Jewish people. It was a magnificent building destroyed by the Romans in A.D. 64. This was the Temple that Jesus knew. In the New Testament Jesus referred to the 'temple of his body'

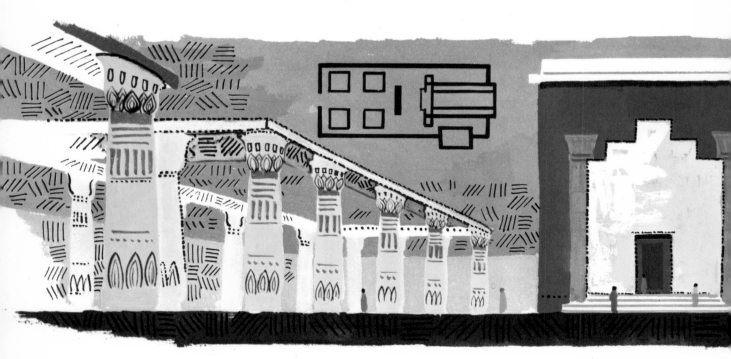

which would be raised from the dead. The Epistle to the Hebrews speaks of the heavenly 'temple' which belongs to all those who regard Christ as their High Priest. *1 Kings 6; John 2. 19–21.*

TEMPTATION. The word 'temptation' in the Bible means to 'test' a person and not, as it has come to be used, to draw someone into evil ways. In the New English Bible 'lead us not into temptation' is more correctly translated as, 'do not bring us to the test.' God tests men in many different ways to show the quality of their faith, and the Lord's Prayer asks for strength to face those tests of character. *Psalm 95. 9; Matthew 6. 13.*

TEN COMMANDMENTS. The 'ten words', or the Decalogue, were given by God to the people of Israel at Sinai and then came to be written on two stone tablets. They contain the heart of God's 'covenant' with the people of Israel and give the basic directions for the keeping of the covenant as a way of life. The 'ten words' are God's words for the people of Israel, a summary of God's law which Jesus himself observed and commended in his teaching. *Exodus 20.*

TERAPHIM. Small clay or wooden objects valued as little 'household gods' or 'idols', and thought to have divine or spiritual power. *Judges 18. 14.*

TERTIUS. Paul's secretary to whom he dictated his letter to the Romans. Tertius puts in his own greetings at the end of the letter. *Romans 16. 22.*

TERTULLUS. The orator who spoke against Paul before the governor Felix at Caesarea. *Acts 24. 1.*

TETRARCH. A name given by the Romans to the ruler of a part of a province. The sons of Herod the Great had Palestine divided amongst them as tetrarchs. *Matthew 14. 1.*

THADDAEUS. One of the twelve disciples about whom very little is known,

Herod's Temple—
its pillared
courtyards; the
Beautiful Gate,
and interior plan.
Inset—Egyptian
style Temple

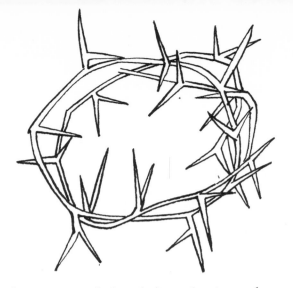

**They plaited a
crown of thorns
to make him king**

but many scholars believe he is to be identified with 'Judas brother of James'. *Matthew 10. 3; Luke 6. 16.*

THEOPHILUS. 'Most excellent Theophilus' is the way in which Luke addresses the man to whom he dedicated both parts of his history—the Gospel of Luke and the Acts of the Apostles. It was customary to dedicate books to a person and Theophilus ('loved of God') was probably a man of culture and standing in Roman society who had made enquiries about the Christian faith. *Luke 1. 3; Acts of Apostles 1. 1.*

THESSALONIANS, EPISTLES TO. These two letters of Paul are the earliest documents in the New Testament. The death and resurrection of Jesus had happened only twenty years before, and there were many Christians who expected that Jesus would appear again soon. This led to the belief that regular work and honest living did not matter very much as the end of the world was near. Paul wrote his letters to remind the Christians in Thessalonica that they should be faithful to this Gospel and be ready for Christ's coming by active work and holy living. They were not always to be looking to the future and neglecting their present duties. *Epistles to the Thessalonians.*

THESSALONICA. The modern Salonika which in Paul's day was already an important sea-port and trading city. The Christian cause there was large and flourishing, and many people of influence and wealth belonged to it. *1 Thessalonians 1. 1.*

THEUDAS. An impostor who stirred up trouble in Judaea after Herod's death just before the coming of Jesus. The Jewish Council in the early days of the church was warned by Gamaliel not to think of the apostles as mere trouble makers like Theudas, and to be careful how they treated them. *Acts 5. 36ff.*

THOMAS. One of the Twelve Apostles. The personal references to him come only in John's Gospel. He did not believe in the resurrection until he had seen Christ personally and touched his body. He has been called 'doubting Thomas' for his lack of faith without sight. *John 20. 24ff.*

THORNS, CROWN OF. Because Jesus was tried and convicted as 'King of the Jews' the Roman soldiers at the crucifixion mocked him. They gave him a purple robe and a sceptre and crowned him with a crown of thorns—made from plants with sharp spines. *Mark 15. 17; John 19. 2.*

THRESHING-FLOOR. The place where sheaves of corn were threshed to loosen the grain, and to separate the wheat from the chaff. Sometimes a donkey pulled a heavy wooden sled over the sheaves. The threshing-floor was a flat piece of rock or hard clay near the village in an open place where the wind would blow away the dust and chaff. *2 Kings 13. 7; Hosea 13. 3.*

THYATIRA. A city in the Roman province of Asia in what is now Turkey. An important point on the Roman road system and a busy manufacturing city. The fourth of the 'seven churches of Asia'. The Book of Revelation warns the Christians in the city of the dangers of paganism in their social and trading activities. *Revelation 2. 18.*

TIBERIAS. A city on the west shore of the Sea of Galilee which was more Gentile than Jewish. It is mentioned only once in the Gospels, and there is no record of Jesus ever visiting it. Herod Antipas made it the capital of Galilee and he named it after the Emperor Tiberius. *John 6. 23.*

TIBERIUS CAESAR. The Roman Emperor who was in power in Rome during the lifetime of Jesus. He succeeded his step-father Augustus Caesar in A.D. 14 and reigned for 23 years. *Luke 3. 1.*

TIGRIS. One of the rivers which traditionally is said to mark the location of the Garden of Eden. It flows down through the great Mesopotamian plain for 1146 miles to join the River Euphrates 40 miles north of the Persian Gulf. *Daniel 10. 4.*

TILGATH-PILNESER. The king of Assyria who reigned from 745–727 B.C. and extended his conquests to the shores of the Mediterranean including Palestine.
2 Chronicles 28. 20.

TIMBREL. The timbrel, or tabret, was a kind of tamborine held and struck by the hand as an accompaniment to singing and dancing. The sound of the timbrel was always a sign of merriment and rejoicing. *Exodus 15. 20; Isaiah 5. 12.*

TIMOTHY. The young friend and assistant to Paul who was often used by him on special missions. He was born in Lystra of a Jewish mother and a Greek father, and his family became Christian. He went to Thessalonica, Corinth, Ephesus and Jerusalem and proved himself to be a loyal friend and follower of the great apostle, who regarded Timothy with tender affection. *Acts 16. 1–5; 2 Timothy 1.*

TIMOTHY, EPISTLES TO. The two letters to Timothy belong to the later period of Paul's life and show the apostle getting ready to hand on his responsibilities to others. They are concerned with the life of the church and for this reason (with the letter to Titus) are called the 'Pastoral Epistles'. They give instructions and directions about the inner life of the Christian communities, and in the second letter Paul speaks specially to Timothy and gives him a splendid farewell message.
Epistles to Timothy.

**Paul to Timothy—
'Attend to your
reading, lecturing and preaching'**

TISHBITE, THE. A name given only to Elijah in the Bible and is probably the name of the area—Tisbeh—he lived in.
1 Kings 17. 1.

TITHES. In Bible times every Israelite was required to give a 'tithe' or 'tenth' of his harvest of grain or fruit and from his cattle to God through the Levites who served the Temple worship. The Levites on whom rested the responsibility for the Temple had no other income and were entitled to receive the 'tithes' and from them to provide for the maintenance of the Temple priests as well. Jesus did not try to abolish the tithe, but he condemned those who were so very careful in tithing but neglected the more important matters of justice and the love of God.
Leviticus 27. 30–33; Luke 11. 42.

TITUS, EPISTLE TO TITUS. Titus, like Timothy, was one of Paul's friends and assistants. He was a Gentile Christian and helped a great deal in settling the troubles of the Christians in Corinth. Paul describes him as a partner and fellow helper and tradition says that he went with Paul to Crete and eventually became bishop on the island. Paul's letter to him is about the organization and life of the church, the kind of people to appoint to office and how Christians should conduct themselves.
Epistle to Titus.

TONGUES, GIFT OF. On the day of Pentecost in Jerusalem the disciples were heard to speak in 'other tongues'. It may have been in 'foreign' languages so that the foreigners then in Jerusalem could understand them. But the disciples may have spoken in such a 'special language' that everyone could understand their preaching. This 'gift of tongues' may be an excited method of speaking which is difficult for listeners to understand.
Acts 2. 1–13; Corinthians 14. 6ff.

TOWN CLERK. One of the neatest and most effective speeches in the Bible is that of the Town Clerk of Ephesus. Following the uproar amongst the people, as the result of Christian preaching, the Town Clerk appeared and spoke clearly and forcibly to the crowd. He may have been the president of the city assembly and more than the city's leading civil servant. But his short speech settled the riot. *Acts 19. 35–41.*

TRANSFIGURATION. 'He was transfigured before them, and his face shone like the sun, and his garments became white as light.' In those words Matthew describes the 'transfiguration' of Jesus which Jesus shared with Peter, James and John probably on Mount Hermon. In the vision on the mountain they also saw the Old Testament prophets—Moses and Elijah. This experience displayed Jesus in a new light. He was the fulfilment of the Old Testament, the king of the new kingdom they hoped for, and they heard the voice of God giving Christ his blessing. This experience 'transfigures' Christ, for it links him to the past and forward to the future. *Matthew 17. 1–8.*

TRIBES. The twelve sons of Jacob each gave his name to a tribe of Israel, and as the tribes came into the Promised Land, after their years of wandering, they were allotted a portion of the land. The main division between them was the River Jordan and lots were cast for the exact portion of land for each tribe. Eventually on the west side of Jordan there was a division between north and south, Israel and Judah. Tribal distinctions faded out when the whole people were conquered by Nebuchadnezzar in 587 B.C. and after they came back from exile. *Joshua 13–19.*

TRIBUTE. When a country was conquered in war by another country it had to pay 'tribute' in gold and silver, in goods and property. People too were deported as part of the tribute and became 'slaves' of the conqueror. In the New Testament the word is used as a word for 'taxes' as when Jesus

A forceful speech by the Town Clerk settled the row at Ephesus

was asked whether it was lawful to give 'tribute' to Caesar.
2 Chronicles 17. 11; Mark 12. 14.

TROAS. Founded near the ancient city of Troy and made into a Roman colony. It was there that Paul had his vision of the man of Macedonia who called to him across the narrow strait of sea to come over and help him. *Acts 16. 8–9.*

TRUMPETS, FEAST OF. The first day of the seventh month, *Tishri*, of the Jewish year. It was to be a day of rest and worship when the trumpets of rams' horns were to be blown as a signal to the people.
Leviticus 23. 24.

TRYPHENA AND TRYPHOSA. Two women, probably sisters, mentioned by Paul and noted for their good works in the church in Rome. *Romans 16. 12.*

TUBAL-CAIN. A worker in metals and described in the Book of Genesis as skilled in brass and iron and capable of teaching his skill. *Genesis 4. 22.*

TYCHICHUS. One of Paul's helpers, like Timothy and Titus, who belonged to the church at Ephesus and went with Paul to Jerusalem. He may have been the carrier of Paul's letters to the churches in Colossae and Ephesus. *Acts 20. 4.*

TYRE. The principal sea–port on the Phoenician (Lebanon) coast and long famous for its ships and sea-trade. Its king Hiram was a friend of David and Solomon and contributed materials for the building of the royal palace and the Temple in Jerusalem. Christ visited Tyre during his ministry and it had an active church in apostolic times. *2 Samuel 5. 11; Acts 21. 3–6.*

U UNLEAVENED BREAD (see also *Leaven*). During the Passover feast, when the Jews remembered their flight from Egypt, only bread without 'leaven' or 'yeast' in it was eaten. It was a reminder that their ancestors had made a hurried departure, not even waiting to bake leavened bread. The cakes of

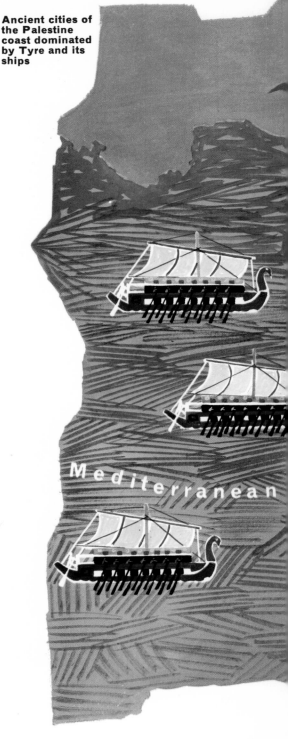

Ancient cities of the Palestine coast dominated by Tyre and its ships

Mediterranean

bread, showbread, displayed in the Temple, were also unleavened. *Exodus 12. 39.*

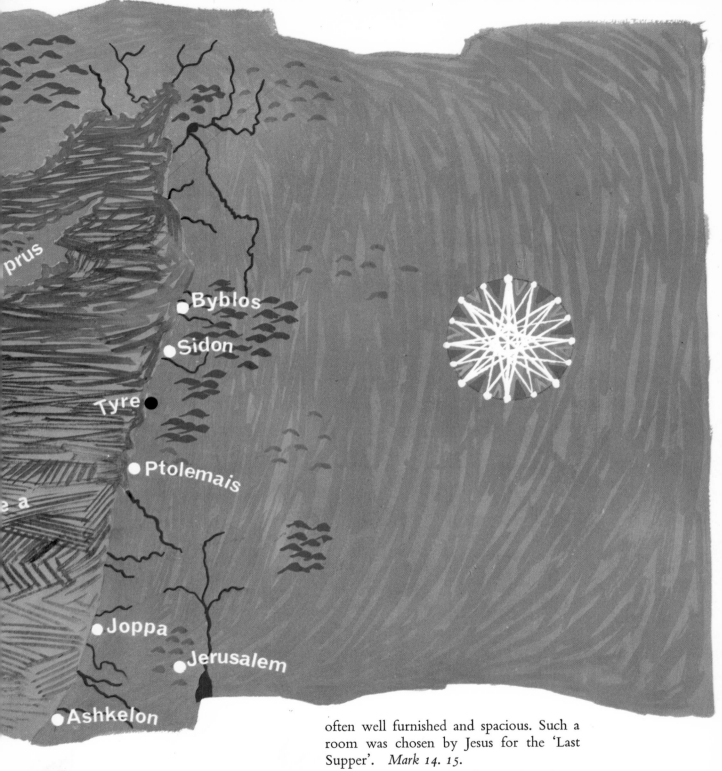

prus

e a

● Byblos

● Sidon

Tyre ●

● Ptolemais

● Joppa

● Jerusalem

● Ashkelon

UPPER ROOM. The 'upper room' in a Jewish home was usually the guest room, often well furnished and spacious. Such a room was chosen by Jesus for the 'Last Supper'. *Mark 14. 15.*

UR. The ancient city of Mesopotamia on the River Euphrates, now in Iraq, from

165

where Abraham set out westward towards Canaan. *Genesis 15. 7.*

URIAH, THE HITTITE. One of David's mighty men. But chiefly famous as the first husband of Bathsheba, later David's wife. David had him put in the front of the battle against the Ammonites in order that he might be killed and so allow David to have Bathsheba.

2 Samuel 11–12.

URIM AND THUMMIM. The Urim and the Thummim were kept in a pouch of the high priest's dress and were probably two 'lots' used in casting lots. They might have been taken out ceremoniously or tossed on the ground. It has been suggested that they were two flat objects kept in the high priest's pocket, which, according to the way they were displayed, could give the answer to questions put to the high priest. *Exodus 28. 30.*

UZZIAH. 'In the year that King Uzziah died I saw the Lord.' The prophet Isaiah begins to describe his great vision of God in this way at the end of the long reign of King Uzziah, who ruled Judah from 783–742 B.C. He began to reign as a boy of 16 and his years were prosperous for his kingdom and righteous in the sight of God. But at the end of his long reign he committed a sacrilege and was condemned to suffer from leprosy for the rest of his life. *2 Chronicles 26; Isaiah 6.*

V VASHTI. The wife of King Ahasuerus of Persia, who refused to appear at his banquet for her beauty to be displayed and was

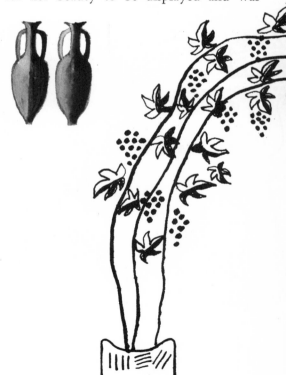

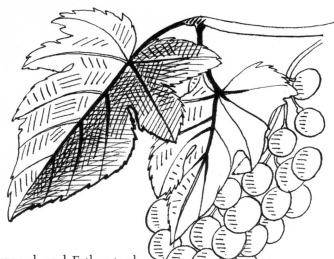

'No more shall be
heard the sound
of weeping ; they
shall build
houses and
inhabit them ;
they shall plant
vineyards and eat
their fruit'
(Isaiah 65)

deposed, and Esther took
her place. *Esther 1. 11.*

VINE, VINEYARD. The
cultivation of the vine and
the care of the vineyard were
among the chief occupations of the Jewish
people in Old and New Testament times.

Jesus healed the
man with the
withered hand
even though it
was the Sabbath
day (see page
170)

The operations of pruning and dressing, gathering and pressing the grapes and bottling the wine, were the regular routine of the vineyard and made up the familiar life of the countryside. Five parables of Jesus refer to the vine and he compared himself to the true vine which has many branches.
1 Kings 4. 25; John 15. 1–11.

VINEGAR. A sour liquid from the fermentation of wine, or other strong drink. It had an acid taste but was drunk by workers in country areas and was also part of soldiers' rations. It was offered to Jesus as he hung on the Cross. *Mark 15. 36.*

VOW. In the Bible a 'vow' is a promise made to God to perform a deed, or to abstain from doing something. A 'vow' is a sacred decision and is binding on the one that vows, and therefore people are warned not to make them hastily.
Genesis 28. 20; Deuteronomy 23. 21–23.

W **WAILING.** At the time of death and burial, much wailing and weeping was expected. It was customary in Bible times to employ professional mourners who beat their breasts, rent their clothes and wailed very loudly. It is clear that Jesus himself did not care for this. At the tomb of Lazarus he wept quietly. *Mark 5. 38ff.*

WATER, WASHING. Water and washing played an important part in Old Testament worship. Before the tabernacle in the Temple stood a bowl of water as a reminder that water was cleansing and that God expected his worshippers to be clean. The priests washed ceremonially before their consecration and on the Day of Atonement. This use of water and washing had its links with the later Christian practice of baptism, or cleansing, and initiation into and membership of Christ's church.
Exodus 29. 4; Hebrews 10. 22.

WHALE. 'Whale' probably means a large fish or great fish or sea monster.
Genesis 1. 21; Jonah 1. 17.

WILDERNESS. A Bible word which stands for any 'desert', 'dry land', 'sandy' place or rock-strewn country. The people of Israel wandered in 'the wilderness' between Egypt and the Promised Land for forty years—first through the Sinai Peninsula, then through the great rift valley extending southward from the Dead Sea, and finally in the wilderness of Zin. In the days of Jesus the wild and mountainous

WISE MEN—see *Magi*.

WITHERED HAND. A 'dry' or 'withered' hand is one in which the muscles have shrunk leaving no life or grip in the hand. Some believe that the modern equivalent is 'polio' or 'infantile paralysis'. Jesus healed a man with a 'withered' hand, even though it was the Sabbath day. By doing so he gave health to the man and new meaning to the day.   *Matthew 12. 10–13.*

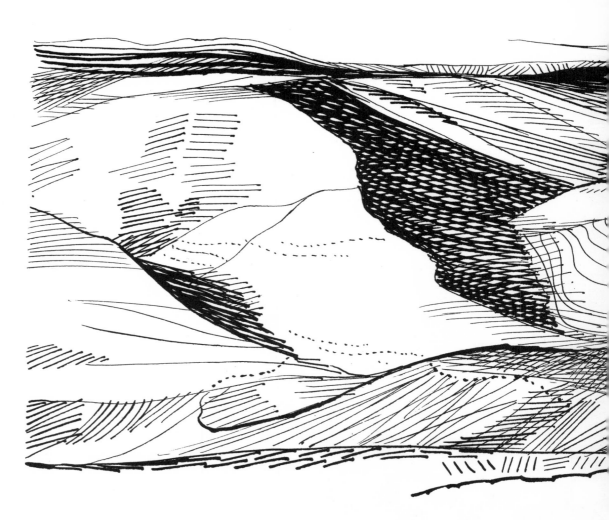

lands east of the Jordan were spoken of as 'wilderness'.
Deuteronomy 1. 19; Matthew 11. 7.

WORMWOOD (see also *Gall*). Many kinds of 'wormwood' grow in Palestine and have a strong and bitter taste. The plant has become a symbol of that which is bitter and sad. *Deuteronomy 29. 18.*

Y **YEAR.** The people of the Old Testament did not have a calendar of the year in the modern manner. They marked the passage of time by reference to the months, the agricultural seasons and the festivals of worship. Their year began in the spring and the Passover (April), and so on through

Wormwood bitter to taste—but pleasant to look at

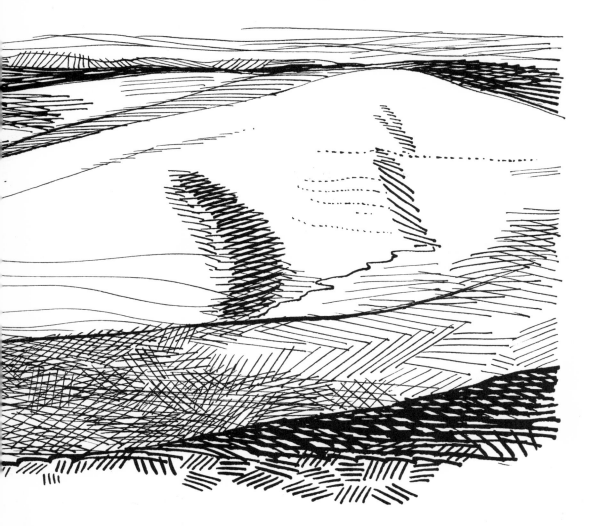

the various harvests of barley, grapes and olives to the end of the year at the citrus

Much of the country that Jesus knew was bare, rocky and sandy—the 'wilderness'

fruit harvest (March). Dates in the New Testament also make mention of the ruler's name as an indication of the time of an event. *Exodus 12. 2; Luke 3. 1.*

YOKE. The 'yoke' was the wooden frame or collar joining two oxen together for pulling the cart or wagon. It is also used to describe how two people, or events, could be linked together. The Book of Leviticus speaks of God breaking the 'yoke of bondage' which kept the Israelites as slaves in Egypt. Jesus speaks about taking his 'yoke' as a sign of dedication to his service. *Leviticus 26. 13; Matthew 11. 29–30.*

Z ZACCHAEUS. 'Zacchaeus, make haste and come down; for I must stay at your house today.' These were the words of Jesus to Zacchaeus the rich tax-collector of Jericho who had climbed into a sycamore tree to

Down came Zacchaeus to give Jesus the hospitality of his home

get a good look at him. Hiding in the branches Zacchaeus—a little man—thought he would see and not be seen. But Jesus spotted him and invited himself to his home. There Zacchaeus admitted that he often got more than he should in taxes and promised to repent and reform his ways. *Luke 19. 1–10.*

ZADOK. Zadok had charge of the Ark for King David, and his descendants were the chief priests in the great Temple of Solomon until its destruction in 587 B.C. *2 Samuel 15. 24ff.*

ZAREPHATH. A small town on the sea coast, eight miles south of Sidon, where Elijah lived to escape the drought in the reign of King Ahab. There he restored to life the son of the widow in whose house he lodged, and who shared with him her last supply of meal and oil. *1 Kings 17. 9.*

ZEALOT. One of the twelve apostles is called Simon 'the Zealot'. It may be that he was given that name because of his zealous character, or because he was associated with 'the Zealots', the patriotic Jewish party who opposed the pagan rule of Rome and refused to pay their taxes. The 'Zealots' were cruelly treated for their loyalty to the Jewish faith and its customs. *Luke 6. 15.*

ZEBEDEE. A Galilean fisherman and father of the apostles James and John who lived near Bethsaida. Zebedee was on the sea-shore with his two sons, mending their nets in their boat, when Jesus passed by and

'Take my yoke upon you, and learn of me'

To pull well animals must be yoked comfortably—so must people (see 'Yoke')

called the young men to join him. They left their father with the hired fishermen and followed him. *Mark 1. 19–20.*

ZEBULUN. One of the twelve tribes of Israel descended from Jacob and his wife Leah. They settled in the Galilee area of the Promised Land where they created a fertile and fruitful countryside. Jesus himself grew up in Nazareth, one of the towns of the Zebulun area.

Genesis 49. 13; Matthew 4. 12–15.

ZECHARIAH, ZACHARIAH, ZACHARIAS. This name is a very common one in the Bible and occurs twenty-eight times. Zechariah, the prophet, and Zacharias, the father of John the Baptist, are the best known. *Zechariah 1. 1; Luke 1. 5.*

ZECHARIAH, BOOK OF. The last book but one in the Old Testament opens with a collection of prophecies and visions of the young prophet Zechariah between 520 and 518 B.C. That was the time of the re-building of the Temple in Jerusalem. In eight visions the prophet describes the blessings that will result from the return of the faithful to the city and the peace and happiness in store for everybody. Some scholars think the last five chapters are not by Zechariah himself. *Book of Zechariah.*

ZEDEKIAH. The last king of Judah (597–587 B.C.). He rebelled against Nebuchadnezzar, king of Babylon and defied him for eighteen months. But in July 587 he could hold out no longer and, with some of his army, escaped and was captured near Jericho. He was carried off in captivity to Nebuchadnezzar who cruelly killed Zedekiah's sons in his presence, and then blinded him. *2 Kings 24. 18–25. 7.*

ZELOPHEHAD. Zelophehad of the tribe of Manasseh had five daughters, and no sons. After their father's death the daughters petitioned Moses that they should have his inheritance as if they had been his sons. This began the Jewish tradition of property passing to a daughter if there is no son. The daughters agreed to marry within the tribe in order to keep the inheritance within the tribe, and so began another Jewish custom. *Numbers 36. 2–9; Joshua 17. 3–6.*

ZEPHANIAH. Prophet Zephaniah lived and prophesied during the reign of the 'good' King Josiah who was only eight years old when he came to the throne in 640 B.C. Zephaniah probably had influence on the young king. His book is concerned with the 'Day of the Lord' and the judgments of God on Israel and the surrounding nations. He denounced the idolatry he saw in Judah and called for a spiritual revival. Josiah led the way for revival by the reforms he brought about, and Zephaniah looks forward to the blessings that God will bring

Zedekiah struggled to keep his independence, but failed morally and spiritually to be a true king

to his people and through them to all mankind. *Book of Zephaniah.*

ZERUBBABEL. One of the leaders of the Jewish people who came back from captivity in Babylon about 537 B.C. to re-build the Temple in 520–515 B.C. *Ezra 3. 2.*

ZIKLAG. A town on the southern border of Judah near the Edomite boundary, and a headquarters for David in the days before he became king. *2 Samuel 4. 10.*

ZIN, WILDERNESS OF. When the people of Israel were approaching the borders of the Promised Land in the last stages of their wilderness wanderings, they came through the 'Wilderness of Zin'. It covered the area between the oasis of Kadesh-barnea and the southern borders of Canaan. Today it is included in the much larger area between Israel and the Red Sea known as the Negev. *Joshua 15. 1–4.*

ZION (see also *Jerusalem*). Zion is often used as another name for Jerusalem. It is a hill at the south-west corner of the city wall which has the traditional sites of the Last Supper room and the tomb of David. Zion was a name also used by the Jews for the Temple itself as the centre of their religious life.
Psalm 147. 12; Hebrews 12. 22.

ZIPPORAH. The daughter of Jethro, the shepherd-priest of Midian, and wife of Moses. She married Moses while he was in the employ of her father and she circumcised their son Gershom according to Hebrew custom—perhaps against her father's wishes. Moses started alone as leader of the Israelites but later Zipporah and their children joined him.
Exodus 18. 1–9.

ZOAR. One of the five 'wicked cities of the plain' at the southern tip of the Dead Sea. *Genesis 14. 2.*

ZOPHAR (see also *Job*). The third of Job's friends who came to comfort him and spoke much plain common sense. *Job 20–22.*

ZORAH. A town in the lowlands of Judah and closely associated with the story of Samson. *Judges 13. 2–25.*

'Your prayer is heard, Zechariah. You shall call your son, John, to make ready a people prepared for the Lord'
(Luke 1. 13-17)

Saint Paul's Travels